Glory RISING

Glory RISING

[WALKING IN THE REALM OF CREATIVE MIRACLES, SIGNS, AND WONDERS]

JEFF JANSEN

DESTINY IMAGE® PUBLISHERS, INC.

P.O. Box 310, Shippensburg, PA 17257-0310

"Speaking to the Purposes of God for This Generation and for the Generations to Come."

This book and all other Destiny Image, Revival Press, MercyPlace, Fresh Bread, Destiny Image Fiction, and Treasure House books are available at Christian bookstores and distributors worldwide.

For a U.S. bookstore nearest you, call 1-800-722-6774.
For more information on foreign distributors, call 717-532-3040.
Or reach us on the Internet: www.destinyimage.com

ISBN 10: 0-7684-3095-X
ISBN 13: 978-0-7684-3095-0

For Worldwide Distribution, Printed in the U.S.A.

1 2 3 4 5 6 7 8 9 10 11 / 13 12 11 10 09

[DEDICATION]

I dedicate this book to the spiritual forerunning mothers and fathers of our faith who were incredibly persecuted for demonstrating the power of the Kingdom of God in unusual miracles, signs, and wonders. These forerunning mothers and fathers willingly sacrificed all in the midst of religious misunderstanding and upheaval in order to reveal the mysteries of the secrets of our supernatural inheritance in the Kingdom of God. I also dedicate this book to my beautiful wife Jan whose sacrifice, faith, and dedication has kept us on track...I love you, baby! And I dedicate this to my children, who will walk in our footsteps. Thank You Jesus for Your great love and presence. We are the best of friends!

Blessings to all of you!

JEFF JANSEN

[ACKNOWLEDGMENTS]

I would like to acknowledge Shae Cooke for her endless hours, hard work, and dedication in the forming of this book. Thank you for working tirelessly in the midst of so much to make this book happen. And to Global Fire Ministries staff writer and editor Eric Green for his contribution in helping to fill in the blanks and putting finishing touches on this project. Without you it could have taken so much longer; you were a lifesaver. A special thanks to all the intercessors and staff at Global Fire Ministries for being such a great source of strength and encouragement to Jan and myself as we tirelessly cross the globe in preaching the Gospel, trying to balance ministry and family life. We sincerely thank you.

I am deeply thankful and appreciative to my children for their understanding of ministry life and giving up of their dad. Thanks Keenan, Hannah, James, John, Philip, and last but not least, Mercy Rain.

Thanks to Mom and Dad Jansen for consistent love. A million thank yous to Jan and Mercy Rain for your understanding hearts and selfless love in sharing me with so many. I'm looking forward to "less being more." There are so many ministry friends and family that I would like to thank personally, but to go down that road would take far too long, and I'm sure I'd leave someone out.

There are many theologians, revivalists, and wonder-workers who I am eternally grateful for and who have forever changed my life through their ministries, writings, and testimonies of great faith. Here are but a few: William Branham, A.A. Allen, E.W. Kenyon, A.W. Tozer, Ruth Ward Heflin, Maria Woodworth-Etter, Dr. Paul Yonggi Cho, Watchman Nee, T.L. Osborn, Smith Wigglesworth, Billy Sunday, Charles Price, Kenneth Hagin, Kathryn Kuhlman, John G. Lake, Aimee Semple McPherson,

John Knox, John Calvin, Charles Spurgeon, Evan Roberts, St. Teresa of Avila, Mary of Agreda, Roland Buck, Joseph of Cupertino, St. Anthony of Padua, St. John Bosco, Cornelius Jansen.

Lastly I would like to thank Destiny Image for your hard work in the publishing of this work. Thanks for moving outside the realm of the accepted norm to present a supernatural Gospel to the world as reality in the Kingdom of God. We love and appreciate you much.

[ENDORSEMENTS]

Glory Rising invites us into our role as sons and daughters of the King and heirs of the Kingdom. Through our fellowship and partnership with God, we actually release Heaven into the earth. The stories of the mystics in Church history and the present-day supernatural encounters release a hunger for what God is making available for us. The author also provides us with valuable tools for having a renewed mind and how our thanksgiving and high praise attract the Glory. This book will challenge you to go after greater levels of supernatural experiences and a greater infilling of the Holy Spirit. The pursuit will impact and change the earth around us as His Glory is released through our alignment with Heaven.

BILL JOHNSON
Senior Pastor, Bethel Church, Redding, California
Author, *When Heaven Invades Earth* and *Face to Face with God*

Jeff Jansen is like a supernatural tour guide into the fourth dimension. His book, *Glory Rising,* reads like a multigenerational map of the heavenly realm. Jeff invites us to join him on an amazing exploration into a fresh spiritual state of consciousness. As you experience the pages of this manuscript, you find yourself overcome with a new sense of God's presence. Whether you are bored in your Christian walk or you just want to reach the stars in Christ, this book is for you.

KRIS VALLOTTON
Co-founder, Bethel School of Supernatural Ministry
Redding, California.
Author, *The Supernatural Ways of Royalty* and
Developing a Supernatural Lifestyle

In this generation, God is raising up new voices with a fresh spirit of faith upon their lives who dare to take the Body of Christ where we have never been. One of these new anointed vessels is my dear friend named Jeff Jansen with Global Fire Ministries. It is my delight and pleasure to commend to you this contagious ministry and the writings of Jeff and Jan Jansen.

JAMES W. GOLL
Founder, Encounters Network and Prayer Storm
Author, *The Seer, Angelic Encounters, Prayer Storm,*
Praying for Israel's Destiny, and many others

Jeff is releasing a clarion call to divine encounters with the Living God, calling the generations to arise and take hold of their unique destiny. In this book Jeff shares wonderful truths that will provoke you to go deeper in the Lord. Your life will be challenged as well as refreshed by these insights into the supernatural power of God. I recommend you read this book as it will encourage your life.

BOBBY CONNER
Eagle's View Ministries

Many think they can only experience the Kingdom of Heaven when they die, but Jeff Jansen teaches you how to be normal. It is normal to experience God's Kingdom now.

SID ROTH
Host, *It's Supernatural!* Television Program

This book will change your perspective on Christian living forever! Jeff Jansen has beautifully articulated the Kingdom principles and supernatural ways that are available to all who hunger and thirst after righteousness. This book has the potential to challenge your spirituality to rise to the next level in God and walk in the power of the glory generation!

JOSHUA AND JANET ANGELA MILLS
New Wine International
Palm Springs, California

I recommend this book to everyone who is hungering for Psalm 63: *"I long to see Your glory and power in the sanctuary."* I know Jeff personally and have had the joy of ministering with him many times in meetings and conferences. As Jeff ministers, a Glory river flows that releases breakthrough and power for all those who are hungry for the Lord. As Jeff shares insight and revelation on the Glory of Lord and His Presence, I know you will be blessed. Get ready to come into agreement with the statement "Fill this Temple with the Glory!" We are the temple of the Holy Spirit, filled with the Glory!

KEITH MILLER
Author, *Surrender to the Spirit*
Stand Firm World Ministries

Jeff Jansen is the "real deal." I have known Jeff for several years and have directly experienced the substance of Heaven that he carries on in his life. By reading this book you will experience no less. Within this book you will not only receive fantastic, forerunning revelation about what God is doing in this hour of history, but you will also receive an impartation of the very substance of God! Jeff Jansen is called to break the Body of Christ into something fresh and glorious, and I believe this book is loaded with enough revelation and presence of God to break you into a fresh new season of God's glory presence in your life! Soak it up and enjoy!

RYAN WYATT
Abiding Glory Ministries

Author Jeff Jansen has done a remarkable job revealing mysteries of the Kingdom in his book, *Glory Rising*. Jeff has had encounters with God which have resulted in every facet of his life being completely changed. His ministry is now marked by God's endorsement of signs, wonders, and miracles. By reading *Glory Rising* and by choosing to live out what the Holy Spirit has revealed in it, you too can become a supernatural carrier and demonstrator of our glorious King and His powerful Kingdom.

Through walking in God's glory you'll become a modern day sign and wonder and a part of this rising Glory generation!

Jason T. Westerfield
President and Founder, Kingdom Reality Ministries

Jeff Jansen's new book, *Glory Rising,* is a must-read for anyone hungering for more of the Holy Spirit in their life. This book will stir you to holy jealousy for the deep things of God, as well as impart a fresh passion to know the King of Glory and see His Kingdom established in the earth.

Jerame Nelson
Living At His Feet Ministries

Jeff Jansen is a true friend of God, and his writing comes from a genuine walk with the living God. This book will inspire you to reach higher, look closer, and taste and see that the Lord is good. It will challenge you to rise above the mediocrity of the masses and join the ranks of the glory revolutionaries.

Charlie Robinson

[CONTENTS]

[FOREWORD]

For many years, Bob Jones and I have prophesied the emergence of a hungry and desperate generation who would seek God wholeheartedly. Bob has called them God's "dread champions" with a heart after God like King David, who also prophesied this reality in Psalm 24 when he said:

> Who may ascend into the hill of the Lord? And who may stand in His holy place? He who has clean hands and a pure heart, who has not lifted up his soul to falsehood and has not sworn deceitfully. He shall receive a blessing from the Lord and righteousness from the God of his salvation. This is the generation of those who seek Him, who seek Your face—even Jacob. Selah (Psalm 24:3-6).

This indeed is that generation of God's sons and daughters who embrace their divine destiny and overcome the spirit of this world to access Heaven and eat from the Tree of Life. A clear mandate has been placed upon this present Church Age to apprehend God's presence and Glory and reveal Him to a needy people.

The Lord will have His harvest, and God's Word will be fulfilled through a yielded and consecrated people who know the supernatural realms of Heaven and walk in its demonstration. We are now seeing the emergence of this reality, and forerunners like Jeff Jansen will introduce the winds of change into this next phase of God's perfect plan.

Through the book that you hold in your hands, Jeff has beautifully captured this prophetic perspective and provides the tools to help us access God's great grace to walk in Heavenly realms and do the greater works. It will be as it was in the days of Joshua, when the Bible tells us that the Spirit that rested upon Moses was imparted to this champion to take his generation across the Jordan into the land of promise.

This book also captures biblical and historical truth showing the convergence of the old and new as described by Jesus when He said:

> *Therefore every scribe who has become a disciple of the Kingdom of Heaven is like a head of a household, who brings out of his treasure things new and old* (Matthew 13:52).

In many ways we must look back at what God has done in order to see what He is going to do. It will be as if we are going "back to the future." In the pages of this book, you will discover secrets to the anointing and walking with God by examining prior healing revivalists and champions. Jeff also teaches us how the blood of Jesus has purchased the restoration of all things going back to the personal intimacy with God and spiritual dominion lost by Adam in the Garden of Eden, as well as how we will walk in these restored realms in the 21st century Church.

Jeff also provides documented evidence of Holy Spirit exploits intended to provoke us to greater heights in God and the affirmation of our messages with signs and wonders. Clearly the early apostolic Church provided a model for spiritual breakthrough and a harvest of souls. The Bible tells us how the Holy Spirit worked with the early Church fathers with the miraculous in order to confirm the message of the Kingdom. It declares in Hebrews:

Foreword

After it was at the first spoken through the Lord, it was confirmed to us by those who heard, God also testifying with them, both by signs and wonders and by various miracles and by gifts of the Holy Spirit according to His own will (Hebrews 2:3-4).

Probably one of the greatest gifts Jeff has provided to us through *Glory Rising: Walking in the Realm of Creative Miracles, Signs, and Wonders* is an awakening of faith to believe for the miraculous and see God's Word demonstrated with power. Seeing the evidence of the Glory realms provokes us into desperation for more. This provides a heavenly atmosphere for miracles, signs, and wonders, fulfilling the words of Jesus when He said, *"Your Kingdom come. Your will be done on earth as it is in Heaven"* (Matt. 6:10 NKJV).

Bob Jones has said, "Something has been imparted to Jeff to help mobilize today's champions to supernaturally cross over into the fullness of God's power and Glory and walk in the 'mantels' demonstrated in the prior generation; the spirit of understanding is on Jeff to forerun something fresh and new."

One of the most impressive attributes Jeff has illustrated in his book is an ability to capture what have previously been considered deep, mystical realities of the Spirit and articulate them in clear, concise, and understandable ways that make them seem readily accessible. God is not looking for golden vessels or silver vessels, but yielded vessels willing to devote themselves and the gifts of the Spirit to build His Kingdom, not their own. This is the clear perspective outlined in the pages of this book.

PAUL KEITH DAVIS
White Dove Ministries

BOB JONES
Bob Jones Ministries

[INTRODUCTION]

Toward the end of his book *Prince Caspian,* C.S. Lewis has Aslan reveal Caspian's origin to him: "You come of the Lord Adam and the Lady Eve, and that is both honour enough to erect the head of the poorest beggar, and shame enough to bow the shoulders of the greatest emperor on earth."[1]

Indeed, we are the offspring of Adam and Eve—God's greatest creation for whom He made everything. We were created as immortal beings and made in His image, and God fashioned us for a much different world, a better place than this fallen world. We don't have to wonder who we are, where we're from, or how we're to fit into this world, because God made us to fit into a perfect world. God intended us for Eden, the garden of delight.

Simply knowing that there is this perfect place helps us know that this world is a broken place, an abnormal world. Knowing that there was a time before the fall of humanity when there was perfect fellowship, communion, and harmony with God and with each other helps us understand who He intended us to be.

What great and extraordinary things could we accomplish if we lived today, in this fallen world, as we will live when supernatural Eden blooms again? God intended us for a supernatural, eternal existence; so why do we try to fit into a place never intended for us?

Though this world is fallen, it isn't worthless because it belongs to God—the earth is the Lord's and everything in it (see Ps. 24:1). He created it, and it was good, and it is worthy of restoration. Though we don't fit into it, we do fit into a supernatural life of heavenly substance in the sight of God our Creator and as active participants in the restoration of all things. As spiritual beings, we live our lives on a stage before angels and demons and the Lord of the universe in a supernatural dimension.

The Bible yields insight and perspective on what we should believe, have access to, and embrace in the divine, supernatural realm of Glory and also what we should reject as false (what satan has perverted) regarding the supernatural dimension of life.

Over the past few years especially, there have been amazing and, to some, unbelievable testimonies of tangible outward manifestations of God's Glory such as gems, gold dust, angelic feathers, and water turning into wine, as well as third-Heaven encounters, angelic visitations, seer gifting, translations, and transportations.

My aim is not to promote the chasing of divine manifestations or divine supernatural encounters or experiences, but to encourage Spirit-filled believers to be open and obedient to what God is doing right now and to what He wants to do in sending Glory revival through a supernatural Church.

The Bible assumes and asserts the reality of a supernatural realm, but our modernistic society has ingrained within us a skeptical mindset that it's not real, it's illegitimate, or it's not for us today. Consequently, mainstream Christianity tends to dismiss the authentic supernatural things of God (supernatural experiences, power, ability, encounters, and outward or tangible manifestations of His Glory) to evangelistic endeavors or to the biblical eras of the apostles, Enoch, Elijah, Gehazi, and others. In a way we've played down and even suppressed its activity, perhaps in fear or misapprehension of breaching "legal" spiritual boundaries. People pray to a supernatural God, but then when He does supernatural things, they attribute it to the devil.

Yet almost one third of the Scriptures involve dreams, visions, and

God communing with His people. A growing number of Christians today are experiencing God in this way—speaking, seeing, feeling, and even doing things with Him in the spiritual realm. These acts and experiences of intimate communion will spur the next great Glory revival, for God says, in the last days,

> ...*I will pour forth of My Spirit on all mankind; and your sons and your daughters shall prophesy, and your young men shall see visions, and your old men shall dream dreams...* (Acts 2:17).

For the most part, we've had a theologically informed worldview that has seamlessly matched reality. But God has called us to that place of heavenly perspective, the Glory realm, and the reality of the supernatural in our daily lives. It's a radical shift from an earthly perspective to a heavenly one.

As God's children, *imago deo,* made in His image and likeness as spiritual beings, we have similar faculties of mind, will, and emotion to the Father. Like begets like, so in truth, each one of us has the potential to walk, live, and have our being in the supernatural ways of God in order to fulfill our mission and very purpose for being here.

> *Those who sow in tears shall reap in joy. He who continually goes forth weeping, bearing seed for sowing, shall doubtless come again with rejoicing, bringing his sheaves with him* (Psalm 126:5-6 NKJV).

It all started in a garden where God placed His newly created son, and it was in that garden that he fell from the Glory of God. So it was in another garden, far removed from Eden, where Christ wept with great tears and agony that would restore humankind back to the original place from which we fell—from the Glory! However, He wept for the joy that was set before Him, interceding for us, sowing in tears, knowing that

His weeping would bring forth great seed of Kingdom harvest. For the joy that was set before Him, He endured the Cross (see Heb. 12:2). The joy set before Him is us.

We are at a time, right now, when God is reaping the very thing Jesus sowed in seed form in the Garden—His offspring, who are doing the very works of the Kingdom of God. Jesus shed His blood for this very reason, and the Father is overjoyed in seeing His children bringing back sheaves of harvest and generating fruit born out of His suffering.

It is the Father's good pleasure to give us the Kingdom. The return of the Glory of the Lord is at hand, and it's time for us to step into high places and into our inheritance, which we can begin living in now.

JEFF JANSEN

Endnote

1. C.S. Lewis, *Prince Caspian: The Return to Narnia* (New York: Collier Books, 1951), 211-212.

CHAPTER 1

ACCESS TO EDEN

As Spirit-filled believers with our roots in Eden, we should live our lives as we will live eternity. Creator God at great cost has opened the way back to Eden, which, for every believer, should be a true view of supernatural reality.

Eden (Hebrew *–dhen*), meaning "delight," was a place of fellowship with God, a place of physical and spiritual delight, and a place of enjoyable occupation.[1] The atoning sacrifice of Jesus provided not only for the salvation of humanity, but also for the restoration and reconciliation of the whole creation, even *exceeding* the glories of the original creation (see Col. 1:20).

God's desire is to have a people who will rightly display and secure His Glory and the power of the Kingdom of God throughout the world. Indeed, this is what we were created for—to secure the Glory of God in Heaven. "This one thing I do" is why we were born, and it should be an enjoyable and delightful occupation (see Phil. 3:13-14).

Our occupation as God's spiritual children is to carry the Kingdom of God everywhere we go. Jesus displayed this as the first of a new breed of Man. He was a Spirit-filled Son of God who role-modeled what we were to do as Spirit-filled sons and daughters of the Kingdom.

The Lord is looking for His Church to keep its head focused in the heavens above and its body fixed on the earth below, walking out the Kingdom mandate with all-convincing demonstrations of His power. To do this, we must reconnect with the Head (Jesus Christ), the *last Adam*, and grow up spiritually (see Eph. 4:15).

The Concept of the Kingdom

The concept of a Kingdom *originated* in the mind of God and *began* in the Garden of Eden. It was in the heart of God to have a royal family of sons and daughters, a community of humanity who would love Him and daily walk with Him in relationship, extending the blessings of that close communion with Elohim to all of creation. Humans were to fill the earth, subdue it, and rule over it, sharing God's rule and reign in kingly authority.

> *Then God said, "Let Us make man in Our image, according to Our likeness; and let them rule over the fish of the sea and over the birds of the sky and over the cattle and over all the earth, and over every creeping thing that creeps on the earth"* (Genesis 1:26).

The essence of a Kingdom is property. Humankind cannot govern something that isn't there. Property or land validates and defines a king or ruler and gives one the right to claim kingship or rulership. Thus, God created the Kingdom territory or colony called "earth" before He created people. God is ultimately sovereign over all by right of creation and ownership. He created humans to be legitimate rulers *as His legal representatives* over this physical Kingdom territory, giving them dominion over the earth (see Ps. 8:6).

Adam, the Firstborn Son of God

God the Father raised Adam from the ground by His supernatural breath. Adam walked in the full measure of his position as a glorified son of God, and God talked with him in Eden in the cool of the day about His divine laws and about Adam's newly appointed position as a co-ruler. When the Father breathed into Adam's nostrils the breath of life, the DNA of the Creator was deposited into his spirit, soul, and body. Adam, with the Spirit of God in him, was created a supernatural being with the ability to create and co-create with God by the power of the Spirit.

Adam, as the firstborn son of God, was completely natural and supernatural. I believe he had a dual nature with full access to the unseen realm as well as the physical realm. It is impossible to know the full extent of Adam's abilities, but it is likely that he had wisdom, understanding, revelation, strength, and power far superior to any person who has ever lived. Above all of his capabilities, his most valuable and precious one was that of knowing, loving, and obeying his Creator. He knew God, and his love for God was pure, his obedience to God unfailing, and thus his joy and happiness freely and naturally flowed.

For a while, Adam was incapable of suffering—he was immortal and nothing could taint his joy. He was God's offspring, a son of His love, fruit of His own nature, created in His image. He was an authoritative son and functioned *in the full power* of this government of the earth as co-ruler, prince, and governor. The greatest model of governor or ruler in the Old Testament *was* Adam, for he was the first man God sent to earth as His representative. This first Adam's government of the earth was in its purest form, as was his relationship to the ultimate power of the cosmos.

God gave to Adam perfect powers and capacities, inherent power and ability. His faculties were supernatural, and therein Adam was more than capable and qualified to govern over every living thing that moved upon the earth—over everything that God had made by the works of His hands. Adam was the conduit between God and creation.

For a season, Adam's relationship with God was perfect and pure, unhindered and full. His was a perfect existence. God genetically engineered him with *perfect* spiritual DNA—DNA unsullied and never touched by sin. While we were birthed into sin, Adam was not, so sin did not obscure or dilute his spiritual senses until he rebelled against God.

Adam's naming of the animals called for a high level of revelation and discernment because the fate and the future of every living creature resided in Adam. The name of each animal would define the species' very nature. Whatever Adam said they were was the nature they assumed. As His offspring, God called him to call those things that are not as though they were (see Rom. 4:17). God did not tell Adam what to name the animals, but gave him the breath and the authority to name them, calling into existence their very natures and purposes.

When God breathes out His Word, things happen. Things come into being because He calls them by the breath of His mouth, and so it was with Adam. For instance, light came into being and solved the problem of darkness when God called for light. That very same breath that breathed into Adam's nostrils is the same breath by which God breathed out His Word and caused things to be. The worlds, the Bible says, were framed by the Word of God (see Heb. 11:3).

This power bestowed on Adam involved great authority and required a unique awareness of the character and nature of God, reverence and awe of God, as well as a spiritual consciousness. This was possible only because of the pure spiritual DNA that resided in him.

When Adam rebelled against God, however, he abdicated his governorship-regency, essentially passing it to the devil by default because the devil had no rightful claim or authority to take it. Adam's refusal to comply with God's instructions regarding the two trees actually *deprived* his human mind of access to godly knowledge and spiritual things and confined it to the pursuit of physical knowledge. Humankind has gained and applied much physical knowledge since the days of Adam. However, government involves the *application* of spiritual principles to be genuinely successful by those governing or ruling, and likewise, by those being ruled.[2]

The Last Adam

Thus it is written, the first man Adam became a living being (an individual personality); the last Adam (Christ) became a life-giving Spirit [restoring the dead to life] (1 Corinthians 15:45 AMP).

God's plan for the earth and for us did not change. Immediately, He set His plan in motion to restore the Kingdom to us and sent Jesus to get it all back for us. The last Adam, Jesus, experienced God in the same pure way the first Adam did. The difference was that Jesus Christ obeyed the Father, kept God's commandments, resisted satan, and never allowed the sinful human nature to enter Him, thus preserving the purity and fullness of that perfect spiritual DNA.

What Adam lost in the garden, Jesus Christ reopened and regained, and He has given it back to humankind. Jesus became Adam again to successfully inject the full DNA of God's original intent back into the earth and our lives so that *we* can now walk in it. Jesus took dominion over the earth, called those things that are not as though they were, and multiplied His disciples. And the disciples later turned the world upside down. Jesus communed with the Father regularly, performed creative and re-creative miracles, effected signs and wonders, subdued His enemies, and in His final awesome and great act of dominion and ruling on earth, conquered death. This immortality is a testimony to us of what the first Adam's life was to be in that ancient garden, and what ours is to be now—a perfect, supernatural existence in relationship with God the Father, the Creator of the Universe.

Reconnected to Eden

And God purposed that through Him all things should be completely reconciled back to Him (see Col. 1:20). What does God want reconciled back to Him? All things. What are "all things"? Everything that was lost in Eden—Kingdom authority, sonship, and the ability to move in the ways of God.

Adam was clothed in light. The Glory of God *clothed* Adam. God wants to walk with us in the ways of Eden as He did with Adam in the cool of the day—He wants us to be clothed in His Glory. Adam was an incredible creation. He moved like the angels of God in the earth. I conjecture that all he had to do was to think about what he wanted to create in the garden and it was done for him. He was a co-creator with God. Everything God created in the heavens and the earth He did with words. Would the elements respond to create matter if Adam spoke them into existence with the authority he had from God? Could he even think things into existence?

God wants us to speak like this again, creating and recreating the world around us in Glory. Jesus Christ paid much too high a price for us to let it all just slip away. He opened up for us the way, which was sealed off in the garden: the Tree of Life—access to Eden. The Father opened up a new and living way for us again through Jesus Christ. This was the original position He created Adam to walk in—access into the presence of God.

Endnotes

1. See Psalm 21:6; 27:4-6; 84:10 and Genesis 2:9,15,19-20.

2. Brian Orchard, "Power to the People," *Vision,* http://www.vision.org/visionmedia/article.aspx?id=137 (accessed December 13, 2008).

CHAPTER 2

THE KINGDOM MANDATE

In this hour, the Kingdom of Heaven is advancing in the earth at an incredible rate. We are beginning to witness the coming forth of past seed sown in humanity—both good and evil. The intercessory prayers made by the saints over the last two millenniums will release a shockwave of the Glory of God in the earth never witnessed in the history of human-kind. As this happens, we will see a massive Kingdom shift that will result in the harvest coming with alarming demonstrations of supernatural signs, wonders, miracles, healing, and deliverance. The Body of Christ is coming into a unity in the Spirit that will grow into a maturity in the full knowl-edge of Jesus, arriving at the complete and total measure and stature of the fullness in Christ (see Eph. 4:13). In order for this to happen, we must know the power of the Gospel we preach and what our mandate is.

What Gospel?

There have been many attributes and truths about the Kingdom that have been preached throughout the ages, with a great deal of success manifesting certain Kingdom realities in power. Each of these truths is essential for establishing the Kingdom on the earth. Even today there are many truths being preached: salvation, deliverance, healing, miracles, and so forth. These are wonderful within themselves, but they alone are not the Gospel of the Kingdom of God.

It's important for us to understand that Jesus did not come preaching salvation, nor did He preach miracles, deliverance, or healing. Jesus came preaching the Gospel of the Kingdom, and as He did, He manifested deliverance, healing, signs, and wonders. The majority of His parables were about the Kingdom of God. As a matter of fact, Jesus mentions or talks about the Kingdom of Heaven or the Kingdom of God 129 times in the four Gospels alone, making it His most talked-about subject. Even after His resurrection, Jesus appeared to His disciples and immediately began to talk with them about the subject that was foremost on His mind—the Kingdom.

> To these He also presented Himself alive after His suffering, by many convincing proofs, appearing to them over a period of forty days and speaking of the things concerning the Kingdom of God (Acts 1:3).

Jesus was saying to His disciples, "Now that everything is set back in order, let's get on with the family business of pushing back darkness and establishing the dominion of the Kingdom of God on earth. This was the reason that I came."

> I must preach the good news of the Kingdom of God to the other towns also, because that is why I was sent (Luke 4:43 NIV).

What a powerful statement! Jesus said His earthly mission was to preach the good news of the Kingdom—this was one of the chief purposes for being sent from the Father. Jesus brought salvation, healing, and deliverance. He performed miracles, signs, and wonders and did it all while preaching the Gospel of the Kingdom of God. When the Kingdom is preached, there should *always* be a demonstration of power. We know this because:

> ...*the Kingdom of God is not a matter of talk but of power* (1 Corinthians 4:20 NIV).

Signs, wonders, miracles, and healings always follow the preaching of the *genuine* Gospel of the Kingdom.

According to Mark, we are commissioned to "Go into all the world and preach the gospel to every creature" (Mark 16:15 NKJV). This being said, it is critical that we know and understand what Gospel we are to preach. We've already established that Jesus, from start to finish of His earthly ministry, preached, prayed, and performed the Gospel of the Kingdom. But what about others in the New Testament; what Gospel did they preach?

In Luke 9:1-2, Jesus gathered the 12 disciples and gave them power and authority to cast out demons, cure diseases, and heal the sick. He then sent them out as apostles, commissioning them to preach the Kingdom of God. After this, Jesus sends out 70 others to heal the sick and say "...*the Kingdom of God has come near to you*" (Luke 10:9).

Paul also preached the Gospel of the Kingdom (see Acts 19:8; 28:23,31). Others preached the Gospel of the Kingdom, like Philip, causing many men and women to be baptized (see Acts 8:12).

The Gospel to the end:

> *This gospel of the Kingdom shall be preached in the whole world as a testimony to all the nations, and then the end will come* (Matthew 24:14).

Clearly, the Gospel that we are called to preach, demonstrate, and live is the Gospel of the Kingdom.

Kingdom Dominion

Your Kingdom come Your will be done, on earth as it is in Heaven (Matthew 6:10).

From time to time I'll hear someone say, "If I only knew the will of God for my life." From the verse above, Jesus made it very clear how to know His perfect will; we can conclude that God's will is *His Kingdom being birthed on the earth.*

What, then, is God's Kingdom? We can break down the word *kingdom* into two words: *king's domain.* The Kingdom of God is the area in which His dominion is established—it's the rule and reign of King Jesus.

God's intent is that His will be done on earth just like it is being done in Heaven—that the physical domain of earth would resemble the spiritual domain of Heaven, as an extension or a territory of the Kingdom of God in Heaven. Another definition for the word *domain* is "a territory over which dominion is exercised; complete and absolute ownership of land."[1] It is a king's territory. God gave us the mandate to rule Earth and subdue, maintain, and transform the planet, with its regions and inhabitants, into a Kingdom territory patterned to look like the Kingdom of Heaven. In short, our mission is to make this place (earth) look like that place (Heaven).

God is industrious. His original plan was to extend His heavenly domain on the earth through a family of sons and daughters—not servants. Servants have no authority and are not part of the Father's house, but serve as subjects in the master's quarters (see Gal. 4:1-7). Sons and daughters, however, have ownership and a legal right in the house to come and go as they choose and to share in all family provision and decisions. The Father's plan was that we would share His rulership as a family of sons and daughters who would rule the earth on His behalf.

Subdue the Earth

The first commandment God gave humankind was to subdue the

earth and have dominion (see Gen. 1:26-30). Adam and Eve's job was to extend the boundaries of the Garden to the ends of the earth. This command, of course, was hindered when Adam fell from the Glory of God and surrendered the earth to the satan. When Jesus came in the flesh, He established a heavenly beachhead on the enemy shores of earth. Through His death and resurrection, He took back the keys of the Kingdom, the authority and rightful dominion of earth, and gave them back to humankind for another shot. Furthermore, born-again children of God around the world have the privilege and capacity to co-labor with Christ to establish and advance His Kingdom in the earth.

Co-laboring with Christ is humans working with God. The Spirit of God lives in us; we are His hands and feet. We are the Body of Christ on the earth today, able to do the works Jesus did—and even greater works (see John 14:12).

We know that Christianity was never intended to be about religion, but relationship. However, there is a legal aspect to true Christianity. Many in the western world don't have a clue about Kingdom operations. Our countries are not monarchies run by a supreme royal authority, but self-governed democracies which originated from the Greek and Roman governments.

In a monarchy, the king and queen have supreme authority over all the land, territory, and people within their kingdom. Everyone within the kingdom looks upon them with utmost respect and honor. They hold all rule and authority—having but to speak the *word* and it will be done. The sons and daughters in the royal bloodline carry that same authority because they are part of the royal family.

We too are citizens of a heavenly Kingdom; a Kingdom not of this world (see Phil. 3:20; John 18:36). Because we are citizens of Heaven, we have a legal right to access all the blessings of Heaven. We know that there is no sickness in Heaven, no disease, no poverty, no depression, no sin, and no broken families. Therefore, we have authorized permission to not only *access* healing, wholeness, prosperity, deliverance, and restoration, but to take those things and *manifest them on Earth*. We are a legal people who have the right of full government and power to rule and regulate planet earth. We are the offspring of God; we have our Father's royal blood and DNA flowing through our spirits.

Jesus is the King of many kings and Lord of many lords (see Rev. 19:16; 1 Tim. 6:15). We are the kings and lords over earth. We are *landlords* so to speak. Heaven is God's territory and earth is humanity's territory. God designed us for the rule of earth, not the rule of Heaven. This also is why we'll return to rule and reign on a new earth.

> *May you be blessed of the Lord, Maker of Heaven and earth. The heavens are the heavens of the Lord, but the earth He has given to the sons of men* (Psalm 115:15-16).

Spiritual Aerodynamics

In His inaugural address to the world, Jesus proclaimed the same words as His forerunner, John the Baptist, "Repent, for the Kingdom of Heaven is at hand" (Matt. 4:17). That message was not only for individuals in and through whom the Kingdom was to be established, but also for the Church, the entire body of believers. It was a call to turn from our old way of thinking and embrace Kingdom thinking because the Kingdom of God is *now.*

The act of repentance is changing our way of thinking from the natural to the spiritual. It is discarding, turning from, and abandoning former thought patterns and processes and adopting the Source of all truth—Jesus Christ. True repentance is receiving the mind of Christ and aligning ourselves (spirit, soul, and body) with the Kingdom of Heaven.

The Kingdom of God is always present tense—it is *now.* The meaning is clear when translating the Greek *engiken* used in the context of "at hand" to the Hebrew equivalent *karav,* which gives us the meaning that the Kingdom of Heaven is "here"—it has arrived. In effect, Jesus declared, "The Kingdom of God has arrived on planet earth. It is time now to change your way of thinking from the old way to the new way, which is the Kingdom way."

Jesus told Nicodemus, a ruler of the Jews, that to *see* the Kingdom of God in operation we must be born from above. What does that mean and what is its significance to us?

> *Now there was a man of the Pharisees, named Nicodemus, a ruler of the Jews; this man came to Jesus by night and said to Him, "Rabbi, we know that You have come from God as a teacher; for no one can do these signs that You do unless God is with him." Jesus answered and said to him, "Truly, truly, I say to you, unless one is born again he cannot see the Kingdom of God." Nicodemus said to Him, "How can a man be born when he is old? He cannot enter a second time into his mother's womb and be born, can he?" Jesus answered, "Truly, truly, I say to you, unless one is born of water and the Spirit he cannot enter into the Kingdom of God. That which is born of the flesh is flesh, and that which is born of the Spirit is spirit. Do not be amazed that I said to you, 'You must be born again.' The wind blows where it wishes and you hear the sound of it, but do not know where it comes from and where it is going; so is everyone who is born of the Spirit"* (John 3:1-8).

Jesus told Nicodemus that in order to *see* the Kingdom of God in operation, he must be born from above. He was saying to Nicodemus that he could never see the Kingdom, nor experience it, unless he was first born from another dimension—a higher dimension. We could also say that we must be "borne" or lifted from above. We must be airborne—lifted from the natural ways of thinking and understanding—into a higher reality. We must depart from earthbound ways, with the intention of being airborne in the heavens. An airplane, as it sits motionless, is bound by the law of gravity, but as it propels down the runway it is lifted into the air. There is another law that comes into play. The law of gravity is bent, because the law of aerodynamics takes over. So it is with the Kingdom of God. The lower laws are no longer in effect or applicable because *lift* begins to occur. We are subject to higher laws—the laws of spiritual aerodynamics.

The Kingdom mindset is superior to the natural mindset. In the verse above, we see that those born of the flesh are born from the natural realm and are *subject to natural laws*. However, those born of the Spirit are spirit and are *no longer* subject to the natural. We can only release Kingdom currency when Kingdom thoughts are thought and Kingdom language is spoken.

The essence of repentance has very little to do with feeling sorry for something bad we've done, but rather turning from our old earthly way of thinking to a new heavenly way of being. Remember, what we meditate on and think about manifests in our lives: *"For as he thinks in his heart, so is he"* (Prov. 23:7 NKJV). We are conformed to the image of what we gaze upon; this is why we are encouraged to fix our eyes on King Jesus (see Heb. 12:2) and to *"...seek first the Kingdom of God and His righteousness"* (Matt. 6:33 NKJV).

> *Therefore if you have been raised up with Christ, keep seeking the things above, where Christ is, seated at the right hand of God. Set your mind on the things above, not on the things that are on earth* (Col. 3:1-2).

In the verse above, we are given a command to *keep seeking* heavenly things—to purposely fix our minds and hearts on things above where Christ is seated and where we are *presently* seated with Christ (see Eph. 2:6). Gaining God's perspective is one of the keys that will bring about the last-day harvest. When we see the world around us with the eyes of Christ, we have tapped into the realm of *all things are possible*.

The Family Business

We can describe the plan of God as simple. It is to extend the rule of His unseen Kingdom or spirit world into the seen Kingdom or the physical world through a family of legal heirs—sons and daughters. These offspring would act as God, on behalf of God, being His legal representatives and judiciaries on the planet, carrying out His orders and implementing His will with full governmental authority given them by their Father and older heavenly Brother, Jesus.

From the dawn of time it has always been about family—about the Father and His children—and will continue to be so until the end days. It's high time for us now to be about the Father's business. After the resurrection, Jesus told Mary, who was the first to see Him, *"...go to My brethren and say to them, 'I am ascending to My Father and your Father, and to My God and your God'"* (John 20:17 NKJV). The word *brethren* can also be translated *brothers.* We are the brothers and sisters of Jesus. His Father is our Father; His God is our God.

Jesus is the firstborn among many brothers: *"For God knew His people in advance, and He chose them to become like His Son, so that His Son would be the firstborn among many brothers and sisters"* (Rom. 8:29 NLT). The only begotten Son of the Father is the prototype for the brothers and sisters who find their way to the Father in relationship with Him and who, with Him, become the heirs of the coming Kingdom. Jesus was not ashamed to call us brothers because we are family with Him. *"As many as received Him, to them He gave the right to become children of God, even to those who believe in His name"* (John 1:12). He gave those who believe in His name the right, ability, and privilege to become children of God.

We are in a place and time where we are starting to see the children of the Kingdom come into maturity. These *seeds* are coming of age and are visibly beginning to bring forth fruit that resembles the fruit of the original *Seed.* Through His offspring, God is manifesting and establishing His Kingdom and His will on earth. He rules the seen world from the unseen world through our spirits, and He births His initiatives through us in the physical realm.

The fruitful journey of Jesus was well documented as He traveled about cities and villages, teaching in their synagogues, proclaiming the good news, the Gospel of the Kingdom of God. He cured *every* sickness, disease, and infirmity that He encountered, further preparing the soil and sowing afresh the precious seed (see Matt. 4:23; 9:35). Everywhere that He preached the zgospel, Jesus manifested His power with wild miracles, signs, and wonders. God expects His offspring, His family, His seed, to do the same works—acting the same way as Jesus did.

> *Because you are sons, God has sent forth the Spirit of His Son into our hearts, crying, "Abba! Father!" Therefore you are no longer a slave, but a son; and if a son, then an heir through God* (Galatians 4:6-7).

Adam's rebellion toward God ended in spiritual death, resulting in him being cut off from access to unhindered supernatural ability and the Glory of God. Adam was left to find his own way in life, filtering the world around him through his five natural senses. But now that which was covered deep in the spirit of humankind has been uncovered by the sacrificial blood offering of our older Brother and Lord, Jesus Christ. It is now being discovered again in this age and time and understood afresh by a family of sons and daughters of God all around the world. All things have been put in subjection under the feet of Christ. We are the Body of Christ—so all things have been put under our feet.

Endnote

1. *Merriam-Webster Online Dictionary*, s.v. "Domain," www .merriam-webster.com/dictionary/domain (accessed March 22, 2009).

CHAPTER 3

CATCHING A GLIMPSE
OF ETERNITY

He has also set eternity in the hearts of men (Ecclesiastes 3:11 NIV).

Throughout the ages there have been many mystical wonder-workers who performed incredible signs throughout the world. These revivalists and mystical wonder-workers were lovesick lovers of Jesus who moved in raw supernatural power that flowed from an intimate union with Christ. This may come as a shock to many who believed that realm was reserved only for a select few during the first century and that with their passing went the miraculous as well. They testify that because we have the complete Word of God, we no longer need the supernatural to evidence the Word. Historical accounts, however, shout otherwise. As we crack the lid of revival history, we find many mighty moves of God's Spirit, men and women of faith and power, and even remnants of believers who carried the call of intercessory and revival fire from generation to generation.

God is still sending ecstatic mystical wonder-workers today to shake and wake the Body of Christ from the status quo into the reality of the realm of Glory. Unearthing these documented accounts buried in the past, we see that there are those who paid a great price to walk in what they possessed. The price, however, was minute in comparison to the Glory that was revealed in and through them.

In order for us to look ahead, it is helpful to look behind. This rising Glory generation has a brilliant future filled with the luminous knowledge and Glory found in the face of Jesus Christ (see 2 Cor. 4:6). One of the repeated instructions given to the children of Israel throughout the Old Testament was to *remember* (see 1 Chron. 16:12). Too easily they forgot the mighty displays of God's power—His wonderful deeds, His miraculous signs, and His supernatural provision.

God wants us to remember. Starting with Jesus, and looking all throughout Church history, we find that these stories of God's mighty hand will cause faith to rise in our own hearts. As we ponder the lives of others who accessed their inheritance and God-given authority, it looses a fresh passion and expectancy for us to seize the promises of God in our own lives, and it launches us further into His unfolding plan of redemption, reconciliation, and restoration.

Jesus, the "Mystic Secret of God"

During His life on earth, Jesus flawlessly modeled to us a natural man in right relationship with a supernatural God. On earth He walked as the Son of Man and not the glorified Son. He was still fully God, but emptied Himself into a body of flesh, becoming fully man. Jesus was *"…made like His brethren in all things"* (Heb. 2:17).

> *Who, although He existed in the form of God, did not regard equality with God a thing to be grasped, but*

40

Normal Ranges for Adult Vital Signs

Temperature	Fahrenheit	Celsius
Oral	97.6°–99.6°	36.5°–37.5°
Rectal	98.6°–100.6°	37.0°–38.1°
Axillary	96.6°–98.6°	36.0°–37.0°

Pulse: 60–100 beats per minute
Respirations: 12–20 respirations per minute

Blood Pressure

Normal:	Systolic 100–139	Diastolic 60–89
High:	140/90 or above	
Low:	Below 100/60	

Annie

MAm

12 yrs old

emptied Himself, taking the form of a bond-servant, and being made in the likeness of men. Being found in appearance as a man, He humbled Himself by becoming obedient to the point of death, even death on a Cross (Philippians 2:6-8).

One of the reasons He was "made like His brethren in *all* things" was to give us an example of what a human being could access, accomplish, and overcome by the Spirit, grace, and power of God.

Before Jesus was baptized in the Holy Spirit, there were no accounts of miracles, healings, or casting out of demons. He didn't demonstrate supernatural feats or multiply loaves of bread for the crowds. He was a Man—a simple carpenter who sought to please His Father in Heaven.

It was after being baptized with the Holy Spirit that His world turned upside down. The doors to the supernatural swung open. Immediately He was led by the Spirit and encountered satan. Angels ministered to Him. He turned water into wine, cast out a legion of demons, and demonstrated Kingdom power. Signs, wonders, and miracles flooded His ministry. We know that we have access to everything Jesus walked in because He was a man in right relationship with God. He even said that we would do greater works than Him (see John 14:12).

Question: *If Jesus was just a man, why was He able to access the supernatural and perform the bizarre wonders that He did?*

Answer: *Because He fashioned for Himself a lifestyle of true communion and mysticism—contemplative prayer and time with the Father. He lived in a New Age—a Kingdom Age.*

Webster's New World Dictionary defines a *mystic* as "one who professes to undergo profound spiritual experiences." It defines *mysticism* as "belief in the possibility of attaining direct communion with God or knowledge of spiritual truths, as by meditation."

Many Christians cringe when they hear words like *mystic, meditation, supernatural, angels, encounter,* and *experience.* Does Jesus fit the above definition of a mystic? Did He undergo profound spiritual experiences, have direct communion with God, and express profound knowledge of spiritual truth? I don't think Jesus fit the definition of a mystic—I think He created the definition! Not only did Jesus model perfectly the life of a true mystic, but He Himself is the very mystic secret of God.

> ...that they may become progressively more intimately acquainted with and may know more definitely and accurately and thoroughly that mystic secret of God, [which is] Christ (the Anointed One). In Him all the treasures of [divine] wisdom (comprehensive insight into the ways and purposes of God) and [all the riches of spiritual] knowledge and enlightenment are stored up and lie hidden (Colossians 2:2-3 AMP).

For too long the occult has claimed words like *mystic, meditation, experience,* and *new age.* Everything satan does is a twisted knockoff of what God does. He takes the genuine and perverts it. He is the ultimate counterfeiter and original imitator. He is jealous of God because he doesn't have creative power; this forces him to rip off of God and do his best to copy Him. The reason he hates humankind so much is because we are made in the image of God. We are children of God, and inherent in our DNA lays creative power. We have a position in eternity that satan longs for, but knows he can never attain.

Poor Christian doctrine states that godly supernatural experiences stopped after the first century. They reach this conclusion not because the majority of their *reasoning* comes from Scripture, but from their personal experience, or lack thereof. "I prayed for someone and they weren't healed; obviously God doesn't heal anymore," or "I haven't seen an angel; evidently people don't see angels anymore" is their mindset. Consequently, they reason that *all* supernatural experiences are demonic. I've even heard Christian leaders say that we should abstain from speaking in tongues. Should we abstain from operating in the gifts of the Holy Spirit—the gifts the Bible says we should desire earnestly and not be ignorant of (see 1 Cor. 14:1; 12:1)?

This type of thinking is hostile toward God and has nothing to do with genuine, faith-based Christianity, only the fear-based scare tactics of satan. In mainstream Christianity, anything supernatural is stamped *evil*. In reality, without the supernatural we wouldn't be here. The universe wouldn't exist; the sons of Israel wouldn't have been delivered out of Egypt; Jesus would never have come in the flesh or risen from the dead. Without the supernatural, the early Church would have taken a nosedive—3,000 people would not have been saved that first day, Peter would not have made it out of prison, and Paul would still be Saul.

We haven't become exempt from relying on God's supernatural provision now that we have the Bible. Somehow we think that we can perfect in the flesh, by our own natural ability, that which was birthed by the Spirit (see Gal. 3:3). We need the supernatural until the Body of Christ attains unity of faith in the full knowledge of the Son of God and grows into maturity. We need heavenly encounters, and we need to behold the Glory of God until we are transformed into the likeness of Jesus. We need the supernatural until Jesus returns with the hosts of Heaven and we are swallowed and consumed by the supernatural in eternity. We are on the road to recovering the true supernatural—with Jesus as our model.

This recent New Age movement has revealed the heart-cry of a generation to truly understand and participate in the supernatural realm. It shows us that mainstream Christianity hasn't stewarded properly the supernatural endowments of God, but denied them altogether. This causes our times of fellowship to be about the dos and don'ts of Christianity. Our sermons revolve more around *sin management* rather than living victoriously by the supernatural ability of Christ in us. Because this radical generation can't quench their thirst for the reality of the supernatural in today's Church, the reality so blatantly found in the Bible, they look to satan. It's time for the Church to arise with a genuine demonstration of power.

The New Age movement is primarily distinguished by a desire for spiritual exploration. There's no covering up the reality of the spirit realm any longer. The majority of the world, and now a large percent of the western world, not only believes in the supernatural, but regularly operates in and experiences it daily. Even the most hardened skeptics have a hard time denying these things, reaching the conclusion that "There are some things we just can't explain." New Agers have no shame in this spiritual journey. They don't care what the path looks like. "There are many paths," they claim. However, we know that Jesus is the only Path—the only Way (see John 14:6).

A large sect of New Agers believe in oneness with nature. They communicate with trees and plants, promote healthy environmental practices, and desire to live in peace and harmony with all of creation. This is simply another rip-off of what Jesus has called us to do—even what He demonstrated Himself. Jesus is the ultimate New Ager!

Jesus spoke to creation on numerous occasions—not only existing in unison with creation, but exercising dominion over it too. In Mark 11:12-14, we see Him cursing a fig tree. Once, on a boat with His disciples, He rebuked the wind and spoke to the sea making it peaceful (see Mark 4:35-41).

Jesus existed in harmony with creation even on a subatomic level—defying what some would call "natural laws." He flew (see Acts 1:9). He walked on water as a man (see Matt. 14:24-26). He walked through walls (see John 20:26).

Jesus is the spoken Word of God. The spoken word is released as sound waves and vibrations into the atmosphere.

> *And He* [Jesus] *is the radiance of His* [Father God's] *glory and the exact representation of His nature, and upholds all things by the word of His power* (Hebrews 1:3).

All things exist and hold together by the Word of God. When we come into agreement with Jesus Christ, harmonizing wholly with the Word of God, we can actually, like Jesus, defy natural laws and display supernatural ability.

Intimacy and Ecstasy

When we behold the majesty of God, our breath is taken away. The beauty of God is captivating. David declared:

I'm asking God for one thing, only one thing: to live with Him in His house my whole life long. I'll contemplate His beauty; I'll study at His feet (Psalm 27:4 The Message).

Mary Magdalene saw the Lord Jesus for who He was. She wasn't concerned with religious activity, but was overwhelmed at being in the presence of her King. She was a lovesick worshiper—consumed with a passion to know Him more. She couldn't help but sit at His feet, in His presence, to allow His words to go deep (see Luke 10:38-42). Imagine the emotion John must have felt when He beheld God on His throne:

Then I saw a great white throne and Him who sat upon it, from whose presence earth and Heaven fled away, and no place was found for them (Revelation 20:11).

God is calling us to a place of intimate ecstasy. We are invited to *"...taste and see that the Lord is good..."* (Ps. 34:8). We are designed to experience God with all of our senses, both spiritual and natural. There is a thirst for the presence of God in the dry ground of every human soul—the heart of a man cannot be satisfied unless it takes delight in the Lord (see Ps. 37:4). The hungry author of Psalm 84 says, *"My soul longs, yes, even faints for the courts of the Lord; my heart and my flesh cry out for the living God"* (Ps. 84:2 NKJV). We are called to dwell in the eternal ecstasy of God's presence and love—personally and experientially. This is the reason Paul bowed his knees on behalf of the church in Ephesus:

> *[That you may really come] to know [practically, through experience for yourselves] the love of Christ, which far surpasses mere knowledge [without experience]; that you may be filled [through all your being] unto all the fullness of God [may have the richest measure of the divine Presence, and become a body wholly filled and flooded with God Himself]* (Ephesians 3:19 AMP).

The past is filled with mystical wonder-workers who intimately encountered God in supernatural ways. These men and women of faith were caught into trancelike visions, raptures, and ecstasies of God's love. They would physically levitate off the ground and even fly. They were taken to Heaven, encountered angels, and were transported, translated, and bilocated!

One of these is **St. Teresa of Avila** (1515-1582). She is one of the many Catholic saints known for extreme ecstatic spiritual encounters.

St. Teresa of Avila

Her life was one of entire devotion to the things of God. Her average day was bathed in contemplative prayer and deep meditation. In these times of quietness she would be overcome by the presence of God and then be swept away into trancelike states.

During one of these visual encounters, she describes an angelic being coming before her and plunging a golden spear with a searing hot tip into her heart. She said that when it was removed, although the pain was severe, it left her totally enflamed with a great love for God.

Many who encountered her couldn't understand her strange behavior; even some of her closest friends declared the raptures she was experiencing were demonic. She, however, continued with her times of devotion and seeking God. Eyewitnesses claim that several times she levitated a foot and a half off the ground for periods up to half an hour.

St. Teresa of Avila is also considered one of the great mystic writers of that era. She penned several great works including *Interior Castle,* one of her final great teachings on the rooms of the soul, and the process of sanctification by relationship with God. In this writing, she talks about the process of four levels or degrees of communion with God. The first, and most basic, is the incomplete mystic union that comes with the quieting of the mind—simple contemplation. The second is the full or semi-ecstatic union with God she sometimes referred to as the "prayer of union." The third level she describes as ecstatic union, or complete ecstasy. The fourth level she depicts is absolute oneness with God—a spiritual marriage between God and the soul.

The Greek word *ekstasis* (ek'-stas-is) is translated into English in the New Testament as "trance," "amaze," and "astonish." *Ekstasis* is defined as "displacement of the mind, bewilderment, and ecstasy." We learn from different passages of Scripture that there are various levels of ecstatic trances. One level is being bewildered and astonished at seeing the miraculous:

> *And overwhelming astonishment and ecstasy seized them all, and they recognized and praised and thanked God; and they were filled with and controlled by reverential fear and kept saying, "We have seen wonderful and strange and incredible and unthinkable things today"* (Luke 5:26 AMP).

Another degree of ecstasy is that of extreme love:

> *Dear, dear friend and lover, you're as beautiful as Tirzah, city of delights, lovely as Jerusalem, city of dreams, the ravishing visions of my ecstasy. Your beauty is too much*

for me—I'm in over my head. I'm not used to this! I can't take it in (Song of Solomon 6:4-5 The Message).

When we go deep into ecstasy, it turns into a trancelike experience. In Acts 10:10, Peter fell into a trance. It was a type of ecstasy where the natural world around him was blurred, which allowed him to clearly see and hear in the Spirit at a heightened sense.

The deepest level of an ecstatic trance is where we become so unaware of our natural surroundings and so clearly focused on the eternal realm, that we're not really sure whether we are on earth, in Heaven, or even in or out of our bodies.

> *...I may as well bring up the matter of visions and revelation that God gave me. For instance, I know a man who, fourteen years ago, was seized by Christ and swept in ecstasy to the heights of Heaven. I really don't know if this took place in the body or out of it; only God knows. I also know that this man was hijacked into paradise—again, whether in or out of the body, I don't know; God knows. There he heard the unspeakable spoken, but was forbidden to tell what he heard* (2 Corinthians 12:1-4 The Message).

All of these types of trances were common in the life and ministry of **Maria Woodworth-Etter** (1844-1924), a traveling preacher during the Holiness and Pentecostal Movements. Some would consider her the grandmother of the Pentecostal movement because she embraced speaking in tongues, trances, visions, dancing, singing, and other outward manifestations of God's presence, including being *slain in the Spirit,* a term that likely originated from her meetings.

On several occasions Maria would be preaching to large crowds and fall into a trance. In the middle of a sentence, with her hand raised, she would stop preaching. Losing expression on her face, she would remain silent for hours at a time. Suddenly, she would snap back into reality and continue preaching exactly where she left off.

Trances were not uncommon for corporate bodies of believers who attended Maria's meetings. The presence of God would flood into the cities where she was preaching, and people would be knocked over under the power of God—even people not attending the meetings! On the streets, in their homes, at the bars. Only moments later they would stand up after encountering God and would be healed from diseases, delivered from addictions, and completely surrendered to Jesus.

Maria
Woodworth-Etter

Below are a few passages taken from Maria Woodworth-Etter's book, *Signs and Wonders*.[1] These are testimonies of just a few things that happened during this Glory Revival described in Maria's own words:

> Five of the leading members of the church said they would unite with me in prayer for the Lord to pour out the power from on high, till the city would be shaken, and the country, for miles around. We prayed that Christians and sinner might fall as dead men; that the slain of the Lord might be many. The Lord answered our prayers in a remarkable manner. The class-leader's little boy fell under the power of God first. He rose up, stepped on the pulpit, and began to talk with the wisdom and power of God. His father began to shout and praise the Lord. As the little fellow exhorted and asked the people to come to Christ they began to weep all over the [church] house. Some shouted; others fell prostrated.

> Divers operations of the spirit were seen. The displays of the power of God continued to increase till we closed the meetings, which lasted about five weeks. The power of the Lord, like the wind, swept all over the city,

up one street and down another, sweeping through the places of business, the workshops, saloons and dives, arresting sinners of all classes.

Men, women, and children were struck down in their homes, in their places of business, on the highways, and lay as dead. They had wonderful visions, and rose converted, giving glory to God. When they told what they had seen their faces shone like angels.

The fear of God fell upon the city. The police said they never saw such a change; that they had nothing to do. They said they made no arrest; and that the power of God seemed to preserve the city.

It held the people still. A spirit of love rested all over the city. There was no fighting, no swearing, on the streets; that the people moved softly, and that there seemed to be a spirit of love and kindness among all classes, as if they felt they were in the presence of God.

A merchant fell in a trance in his home and lay several hours. Hundreds went in to look at him. He had a vision, and a message for the church. The Lord showed him the condition of many of the members. He told part of his vision, but refused to deliver the message to the church. He was struck dumb. He could not speak a word because he refused to tell what the Lord wanted him to.

The Lord showed him he would never speak till he delivered the message. He rose to his feet, weeping, to tell the vision. God loosed his tongue.

One night there was a party seventeen miles from the city. Some of the young ladies thought they would have some fun; they began to mimic and act out the trance. The Lord struck some of them down. They lay there as if they had been shot. Their fun-making was soon turned to a prayer-meeting, and cries of mercy were heard. The people came to the meetings in sleigh loads many miles. One night while a sleigh load of men and women was going to the meeting they were jesting about the trances. They made the remark to each other that they were going in a trance that night. Before the meeting closed all who had been making fun were struck down by the power of God and lay like dead people, and had to be taken home in the sled in that condition. Those who came with them were very much frightened when they saw them lying there, and they told how they had been making fun of the power of God on the way to the meeting. Scoffers and mockers were stricken down in all parts of the house.

One man was mocking a woman that God had taken control of her body. She was preaching with gestures. When in that mocking attitude God struck him dumb. He became rigid and remained with his hands up, and his mouth drawn in that mocking way for five hours, a gazing-stock for all in the house. The fear of God fell on all. They saw it was a fearful thing to mock God or make fun of his work.

Surely, the Lord worked in a wonderful way in this meeting. The postmaster was converted. All classes from the roughs and toughs to the tallest cedars and brightest talents of the city were brought into the fold of Christ. We took the meeting to the opera house and it would not hold the crowds.

The Cincinnati Enquirer sent a reporter to write up the meetings and report daily. Every day the newsboys could be heard crying out, "All about the Woodworth revival."[2]

Maria Woodworth-Etter was arrested and put in prison on several occasions for practicing medicine without a license and "hypnotizing" people with trances. However, these were only looked at as minor hiccups in her life—she continued to press forward and preach until she went home to be with the Lord in 1924. The last few of her sermons were preached from her bed. *Hers was a life of commitment to ministering the manifest presence of God to people*—she was always quick to stop and rest in His presence.

Supernatural Downloads

A trance is a means of being opened to hear God's voice and receive revelation from the supernatural realm of Heaven. A trance is the door through which we access the revelatory realm—the vehicle that takes us into the heavens. In this place of ecstasy, our spiritual senses are heightened and our unrenewed minds take the place of servant instead of master—coming into submission and obedience to the things of the Spirit. In this place of submission, our minds become renewed and receive supernatural downloads of heavenly knowledge, revelation, and wisdom. We become open to receive the counsel of the Spirit.

> *...for the Spirit searches all things, even the depths of God....Now we have received, not the spirit of the world, but the Spirit who is from God, so that we may know the things freely given to us by God, which things we also speak, not in words taught by human wisdom, but in those taught by the Spirit, combining spiritual thoughts with spiritual words. But a natural man does not accept the things of the Spirit of God, for they are foolishness to him; and he cannot understand them, because they are spiritually appraised* (1 Corinthians 2:10,12-14).

One man who received extreme supernatural downloads of revelation was **St. Ignatius** (1491-1556), founder of the Jesuit Order. Once he was seated at the side of a road gazing at a stream that crossed it.

He was absorbed in deep contemplation when suddenly the eyes of his soul were opened and overflowed with light. In this experience he wasn't able to distinguish anything with his five natural senses, but was able to understand marvelously a great number of truths pertaining to the faith and human sciences. It seemed to him like he entered a new world; the new concepts and ideas were so numerous, so magnificent. According to St. Ignatius, the amount of new knowledge was so great, all that he had learned in his life up until this time, his 62nd year, whether supernatural or through lengthy study, could not be compared to what he had learned during this single ecstatic experience.

St. Ignatius

Other supernatural experiences were not uncommon throughout St. Ignatius' life. Once, while recovering from severe sickness, he was lifted off the ground in prayer in the kneeling position. Onlookers heard his prayer: "O, my God, how can I love You as You deserve. If men but knew You, they would never offend You; for they would love You too much to do so."[3]

St. Ignatius was enamored with God—he loved to love Him. During one of the Holy Masses a flame of fire manifested and hovered above St. Ignatius' head. Fr. Nicholas Lannoy, one who was attending the Mass, was horrified and ran forward to extinguish the flame. He was surprised to find St. Ignatius lost in ecstasy with no physical signs that the flame was burning him. He stared in amazement for quite some time.

Another man who received downloads of super-natural revelation, a little closer to our time, was **Roland Buck** (1918-1979), an Assembly of God pastor in Boise, Idaho. During a season of encounters, he was visited 27 times by the angel Gabriel and was sucked up to the throne room where he received supernatural knowledge about the Bible and the nature of God. Burned into his mind were 2,000 Scripture passages that he could quote at any time. When talking

Rolland Buck with his dog Queenie

to him, people said it was like talking to a Bible; his words and ideas were bathed in Scripture. In his own words below, Rolland describes one of his throne room experiences:

One Saturday night in January of 1977, at about 10:30 P.M., I was seated at my desk, meditating, praying, and preparing my heart for Sunday. I had my head down on my arm at the desk, when suddenly, without any warning, I was taken right out of that room!

I heard a voice say: "Come with me into the Throne Room where the secrets of the universe are kept!" I didn't have time to answer; space means nothing to God! It was like a snap of the fingers—boom—and I was right there! Only then did I recognize that the voice I had heard speaking to me was the voice of the Almighty God!

I was nervous, and God told me to relax. He said, "You can't prove anything to me, because I already know you." I began to relax even though it was so awesome I had difficulty comprehending what was happening.

He came right to the point and said, "I want to give you (and this is *His* expression) an 'overlay' of truth." In a split second of eternity, we went from Genesis to Revelation, looking first at God's plan for his people. Throughout all of the Bible, God discussed His character, stating, "I will do nothing in conflict with My nature or My character. My plan for you is good and it will be accomplished."

During this visit, God truly gave me a glorious glimpse of the hidden secrets of the universe; of matter, energy, nature and space, all bearing the same beautiful trademark. As he gave me this dazzling overlay of truth, it added a new beauty and unity to the entire Bible which I previously did not have. Certain biblical truths which I had seen darkly were now perfectly clear, and I could see how all the pieces fit together in what God was doing!

Then God said I could ask questions! My mind was whirling! How does a human ask questions of God? It was so awesome being in His presence I could hardly think. Finally a thought came into my mind to find out whether or not He actually made individual plans for each and every life, because for some reason or other, I felt this gigantic task would be too big even for God!

In answer to my question, God let me see the vastness of his heavenly archives! My head swam! There was no way my finite mind could understand how God could keep track of these files. There must be billions of them! He said, "Since you are overwhelmed by this, and it staggers you, let Me pull out one that you can relate to." And He immediately pulled out mine! He would not let me see the contents of it, but mentioned a few of the future items listed which I could use as confirmation of this visit.

Then he did another very surprising thing! He wrote down 120 events which he said would happen in my life in the future. It wasn't like you and I write; the information just suddenly appeared! I did not even need to read it, but right now, I can tell you *everything* that was on that paper, because it was instantly impressed on my mind like a printing press prints on paper. The press doesn't have to read what is imprinted. It's there! In the same way, every single notation was burned into my mind, and it's still there! Even though I had this knowledge, God also let me know that he did not want me to reveal any of these things until such times as He would release me to share them.[4]

Eventually Roland was released to share the 120 events, each of them coming to pass before he went to be with the Lord. The Lord allowed Roland to peer into eternity and receive but a fraction of supernatural knowledge concerning matter, energy, space, and nature available to believers.

Supernatural downloads of knowledge are not uncommon in the Body of Christ today. There are many others throughout history who have received supernatural knowledge, understanding, and revelation in the realm of Glory, including **Bob Jones** (1930-present), a spiritual father to me and to this generation and a good friend of mine.

Bob Jones

When Bob was nine years old, he encountered the angel Gabriel as he walked home from school on a dirt road in Arkansas. Bob recalls the angel coming out of the clouds on a white horse and then walking up to him on the country road. The angel dumped a large bull-skin mantle on the ground in front of him then pulled out a long silver trumpet and blew it in his face. The angel proclaimed that Bob was called to be a prophet to the nations and then rode away. Bob was terrified and ran home not telling anyone about this incredible experience.

One evening, a few years later, the Lord Jesus came into Bob's bedroom and took him by that hand and brought him to Heaven. Bob recalls everything being flooded with light; the things he witnessed were unimaginable, unspeakable. Bob became so overwhelmed during the experience he asked the Lord to take him back, so He did. After this experience, Bob supernaturally had understanding and comprehension for all of his classes. He knew facts and dates in history that he hadn't previously studied and became a whiz at math without even trying. He received an impartation of knowledge from Heaven and became an "A" student practically overnight. Also imprinted on his mind was a staggering amount of Scripture.

Supernatural experiences like these impact the molecular structure of the brain, causing it to receive information much like a computer receives an upgrade. More frequently, people's minds are being renewed and transformed by these powerful mystical ecstatic experiences.

The Church has told us for years that this is dangerous ground and we should avoid such supernatural practices. I say that because we have shut down this place in God, we are on dangerous ground now. Those who shame these heavenly encounters are actually coming into agreement with the enemy and his demonic attempt at keeping the Body of Christ from receiving revelatory experiences which indeed liberate and advance us forward into our spiritual inheritance.

In the coming days, we will witness an increase in supernatural revelation that will also greatly benefit the sciences. There will be new inventions, alternate energy sources, and the capability of restructuring the molecular makeup all the way down to a single atom. Even now angels are visiting believers, giving them formulas and blueprints to help bring these things about. The unthinkable will be thinkable—the undoable will be done!

Endnotes

1. Maria Woodworth-Etter, *Signs and Wonders* (Tulsa, OK: Harrison House, 1916), 63-65.

2. Ibid.

3. Mary Purcell, *The First Jesuit, St. Ignatius Loyola* (Chicago: Loyola University Press, 1981), 71.

4. Charles Hunter and Frances Hunter, *Angels on Assignment, as told by Roland Buck* (Kensington, PA: Whitaker House, 1979). Online version accessible at http://angelsonassignment.org.

CHAPTER 4

MYSTICAL WONDER-WORKERS
PAST AND PRESENT

*This, the first of His signs (miracles, wonderworks), Jesus
performed in Cana of Galilee, and manifested His glory
[by it He displayed His greatness and His power openly],
and His disciples believed in Him [adhered to, trusted in,
and relied on Him]* (John 2:11 AMP).

When supernatural signs, wonders, and miracles are performed,
they impart to the viewer a fresh vigor to cast off the detrimental
restraints of doubt, fear, and unbelief. They act as a catalyst to propel
them into deeper realms of faith, trust, and reliance in Jesus Christ.

It is the Spirit of God who gives us the ability to move and operate
in Kingdom principles and realities: *"To another [wonder-working faith by*

the [Holy] Spirit, to another the extraordinary powers of healing by the one Spirit; to another the working of miracles, to another prophetic insight..." (1 Cor. 12:9-10 AMP). In this hour, God is pouring out fresh waves of His Spirit, and He expects us to move in supernatural phenomena that gives Him Glory.

In this chapter, as we look at more accounts from the Bible and from mystical wonder-workers throughout Church history, an impartation of wonder-working faith is ready to be manifested in your own life. These mantels are yours for the taking! Jesus said it Himself: *"To you it has been given to know the secrets and mysteries of the kingdom of heaven..."* (Matt. 13:11 AMP). Surrender old paradigms to the Holy Spirit and let Him be your guide in the supernatural Kingdom of Heaven—you'll never be the same!

Translation of the Spirit

Translation is a unique experience where the spirit of a person is actually lifted from their body and is brought to another place by the Spirit of God or sometimes by angels. The occult calls such out-of-body experiences "astral projection" or "astral travel." However, they do this illegally, outside of the guidance of the Holy Spirit and outside of Christ. They forcefully project their spirits to other locations or are guided by demonic spirits. Obviously, doing this outside of Christ is not only illegal, but dangerous. It is another counterfeit to the genuine experiences available to the saints of God. Being translated in the Holy Spirit, however, is legal, safe, and one of the many ways God can speak and reveal the mysteries of His Kingdom to us.

Two people in the Bible who had definite translation experiences were Elisha and Paul. In 2 Kings 5:20-27, we see the story of Elisha's servant, Gehazi, swindling Naaman out of two talents of silver as he was traveling on his chariot. When Gehazi came back to the house, he stood before his master Elisha. Elisha asked him where he had been. Gehazi lied to him and said he hadn't gone anywhere. Elisha said to him:

> ...Was not my spirit with you when the man got down
> from his chariot to meet you? (2 Kings 5:26 NIV)

I'm sure Gehazi realized at that point he shouldn't have tried to lie to the prophet. Elisha cursed Gehazi with leprosy, and he turned as white as snow.

Elisha's spirit was with Gehazi while he was cheating Naaman, and he witnessed the entire event. He was, however, completely invisible to all who were present. Paul mentions similar experiences in two of his letters. He says in Colossians:

> For even though I am absent in body, nevertheless I am
> with you in spirit, rejoicing to see your good discipline and
> the stability of your faith in Christ (Colossians 2:5).

In First Corinthians he says:

> For I, on my part, though absent in body but present in
> spirit, have already judged him who has so committed
> this, as though I were present (1 Corinthians 5:3).

These translation experiences are more than visionary encounters; the spirit of a person is actually present in a different location. During these experiences they have the ability to see and hear the events taking place and gain detailed knowledge of specific circumstances.

Not too long ago I was ministering in a meeting and I began to talk like Bob Jones. As I looked around the room, there in the corner was Bob standing and looking at me. He didn't say anything but stared as though he was checking me out. I saw Bob shortly after that event and told him I had seen him standing in my meeting watching me as I preached. Bob said, "Yeah I know...I check up on all my boys."

Transportation of the Body

Transportation is when the spirit, soul, and body of a person are transported to another location. Unlike translation, where only the spirit of a person travels, transportation is when the entire person is physically transported to a different location. What makes this possible? In the word *transportation,* we see the word *port,* which is short for *portal.* Transportation occurs when a portal opens in the spirit and a person goes through it. These portals sometimes manifest as gates, windows, or doors. The Holy Spirit Himself is a type of portal who can take us places.

There are different levels of being transported in the Spirit. Sometimes a person is taken physically, but is cloaked with invisibility so he cannot be seen. Sometimes a person is completely transported to another location, like Philip, who was snatched away by the Spirit and plopped down 30 miles away (see Acts 8:39-40). And sometimes we are transported into Heaven, like Elijah, who was swooped up in a whirlwind; or Ezekiel who was jerked up between earth and Heaven and had heavenly visions when the Spirit of God grabbed a lock of his hair; or like John when he saw a door in Heaven and heard a voice beckoning Him to come up (see 2 Kings 2:11; Rev. 4:1-2).

Then there are times when we are so deep in ecstatic intimacy, we're not really sure if the encounter we are experiencing is in the spirit or if we are physically present. Paul, speaking of himself, talks about his heavenly encounters and shares that he's not sure if he was in his body or not:

> ...but I will go on to visions and revelations of the
> Lord...such a man was caught up to the third heaven.
> ...whether in the body or apart from the body I do not

know, God knows—was caught up into Paradise and heard inexpressible words... (2 Corinthians 12:1-4).

Unlike the natural realm, there is no distance or time in the realm of the spirit. The worlds were framed from the realm of the spirit—the seen came from what was unseen. The realm of the spirit is very real and is actually superior to the physical realm. The spirit determines the natural. This is why faith is important—it connects us to the spirit realm and allows us to adjust things accordingly, opening and closing doors in the spirit. This, in turn, manifests in the natural. The realm of the spirit influences and controls everything in the physical world. If we change the atmosphere in the spirit, it will alter the physical realm also.

The Wonderful Gift of Bilocation

Bilocation is another phenomenon that is difficult for the natural mind to grasp. Bilocation occurs when a person is present in two places simultaneously. Although there are no instances of this unique manifestation recorded in the Bible, there are numerous documented accounts of bilocation in the lives of the saints.

Bilocation can be categorized with translation and transportation. However, instead of the saint's spirit traveling to a different location, or his entire spirit, soul, and body doing so, bilocation occurs when he is tangibly in two locations at the same time. This, of course, is physically impossible and breaks the natural laws of matter, space, and time. There have been accounts of bilocators going places in the Spirit where they are able to fully interact with people and minister to them. When they've finished the experience they sometimes have physical objects with them that they were holding or had put in their pockets during the experience—physical objects! There are many untapped mysteries waiting to be discovered about the realm of the Spirit. This realm is very real—and these experiences are very real.

Some people believe that when bilocation occurs, it is the spirit of a person being projected and then manifesting physically, taking on a physical substance, fully able to interact with people and objects. Another prevailing theory suggests that the projection is an exact double or replica of the person—how this happens, we're not sure. We know that God is omnipresent and He fills all things. God is able to be in two places at one time. I suggest that because we are made in the image of God, we are fully capable of being in more than one place at the same time.

Bilocation is a wonder-working gift that displays the power of the miraculous and can deepen our experiential walk with the Lord Jesus. However, the gift of bilocation, like any mystical gift, is rarely for the recipient, but to help aid him in performing some type of ministry. As we dive into some of these well-documented stories of bilocators, we will witness them helping the needy, attending the dying, preaching the Gospel, and blessing others.

When explaining supernatural feats, miracles, wonders, and signs, we don't really need to figure everything out. When trying to explain the unexplainable, we take something so holy, so magnificent, so extraordinary, and make it ordinary. If we analyze something from every angle and think we understand it fully, it loses its mystery. There is nothing wrong with studying the supernatural and understanding it. But it becomes wrong when we fail to move past simple head knowledge into personal experience. Sometimes it's necessary to simply give the details of *what happened* instead of feeling the need to explain *how it happened*. For too long the Church has taken the *wonder* out of the *God of wonder*—we've limited God to a box in our unrenewed minds. It is time to believe in the God of the impossible again and to encounter Him personally. In this hour, faith must override our natural ways of thinking—nothing will be impossible for us when we believe (see Mark 9:23). Bilocation is possible for all who believe.

St. Alphonsus Liguori (1696-1787) was seen by credible witnesses to be in two different locations at the same time on several occasions. One time he was seen preaching a sermon in the pulpit and at the same time was in the confessional. On another occasion he was preaching to university students in Naples while a poor woman came to the door at Pagani to accept the alms that were regularly given to her by St. Alphonsus. At the door the woman was met by a lay brother who told her the Saint was in another city and sent her away. Instantly St. Alphonsus was present and gave her the usual amount of money.

One of the most astonishing times St. Alphonsus is reported bilocating is during the death of Pope Clement XIV. The saint fell into a trance after Mass for nearly two days without showing any sign of life. During the experience, he was assisting the Pope during his death. The Rev. Tannoia, a friend of St. Alphonsus, describes it this way:

During the morning of September 21, 1774, Alphonsus, after saying Mass, threw himself in his armchair, as he was not wont to do. He appeared prostrate and absorbed in thought, making no movement, speaking no word and asking no one for anything. He remained in that state for all that day and the night that followed, and all the while took no food and made no sign that he would undress. The servants who saw him in this position, wondering what was to happen, stood by the door of his room, unwilling to go in. On the morning of the 22nd he had not changed his attitude and the household did not know what to think. The fact is that he was in a prolonged ecstasy. Later on in the morning, however, he rang the bell to announce that he wished to say Mass. At that signal, it was not only Brother Romito who came as usual, but everybody in the house ran to the bishop's room. On seeing so many people, the Saint asked in surprised tones what was the matter. "What is

St. Alphonsus Liguori

the matter?" they answered, "this is the second day that you have not spoken, eaten, nor given any sign of life." "You are right," said Alphonsus, "but you do not know that I have been assisting the Pope, who has just died."[1]

Not long afterward, everyone received the news that Pope Clement XIV had past away around 7:00 A.M. on September the 22nd. This was the same time St. Alphonsus came out of the trance.

It is not uncommon to see bilocators attend the dying. Another occasion of this is in the life of **St. Joseph of Cupertino** (1603-1663)

who bilocated to assist an elderly friend during his death. The elderly gentleman, Octavius Picinno, who was affectionately called "Father," asked St. Joseph if he would assist him at the hour of his death. The saint agreed and added, "I shall assist you, even though I should be in Rome." Indeed, while St. Joseph was in Rome, Octavius became sick. During the last

St. Joseph Cupertino

hour of his life, those caring for him saw St. Joseph speaking with him. Sr. Teresa Fatali of the Third Order was present and asked the saint how he got there. "I came to assist the soul of 'Father,'" was his response, and then he suddenly disappeared.

The second occasion recorded of St. Joseph bilocating is when he assisted his mother during her death. On her deathbed in Cupertino, St. Joseph's mother realized she wouldn't have the opportunity to be with her son again and cried out, "Alas, my dear Joseph, I shall not see you again." At this time the saint lived in Assisi, but suddenly appeared in the room after a bright light flashed. He stood next to his dying mother who shouted, "O Father Joseph! O my son!" During this same moment at the church in Assisi, Fr. Custos asked St. Joseph why he was weeping with sadness. The saint replied, "My poor mother has just died." A few days later a letter arrived stating that the saint's mother had passed away. The witnesses solemnly testified that St. Joseph of Cupertino was present and assisted his mother on her deathbed.[2]

Not only did St. Joseph bilocate, during his life he also levitated and flew over 70 times, performed numerous miracles, and was often sought by others to give advice and answer complex questions. However, he was often considered a mindless misfit because of the abundance of ecstatic raptures he experienced. He would only have to start thinking about the Lord or hear music and he would begin to float off the ground. Because of these strange occurrences he wasn't allowed to attend public mass for 35 years, but was often confined to his room with a smaller chapel. He was sold out to God and showed his passion for the Lord by regularly fasting and surrendering his life to continual worship and prayer.[3]

One of the most astonishing cases of bilocation recorded is in the life of the **Ven. Mary of Agreda** (1602-1665), a nun who lived in a convent for 46 years in Agreda, Spain. Also known as Maria of Agreda, she not only bilocated across Spain and Portugal, but also crossed the Atlantic to visit America.

In 1620, while immersed in ecstatic prayer, Maria was transported to New Mexico where she was commanded by the Lord Jesus to teach the Indians. Immediately she began to teach them about the Lord and the things pertaining to the Catholic faith. Although she spoke

Venerable Mary of Agreda
"Lady in Blue"

her native language of Spanish, the Indians understood her perfectly and she could understand them as well. The Indians called her the "Lady in Blue" because of the blue mantle she wore. Later, when she awoke from her ecstasy, she found herself back in Agreda at the convent. Over the next 11 years, from 1620 to 1631, Maria bilocated over 500 times, sometimes making as many as four visits in one day!

The Archbishop of Mexico, Don Fransisco Manzo Y Zuniga, began receiving reports from missionaries who said that the Indians sought them out under the direction of a lady in blue. The Archbishop put Fray Alonzo of Benavides of the Franciscan Order in charge of investigating the matter on a deeper level.

Sitting outside the Isleta Mission in 1629, Fray Benavides had a group a 50 Indians approach him and ask for missionaries to come to their territory. The Indians had traveled a great distance from Titlas, or Texas, under the direction given by a lady in blue; they knew exactly where to find the friars and the Isleta Mission. Two missionaries were sent back with the group of Indians, and upon their arrival they found the rest of the Indians well instructed about faith in Jesus Christ and willing to be baptized.

Finally, after 11 years of searching, Fray Benavides located the mysterious nun in Agreda, Spain. Out of humility Maria wouldn't share about her experiences. Later she was ordered under the authority of Fr. Bernardine of Siena, the Superior General, to share everything about her trips to America. She was questioned by Fray Benavides in the presence of her confessor about the various oddities of the province in New Mexico. She was able to clearly describe the nature and climates of the province, the many unique customs of the different tribes of Indians, as well as other numerous details. By the many unique details of her journeys, Fray Benavides was entirely convinced that she was speaking nothing but truth.

Later, Maria was given a thorough ecclesiastical examination by Fr. Anthony da Villacre, the Provincial of Burgos. He declared that her mystical favors were indeed authentic.

A doctor in theology, J.A. Boullan, wrote of Maria, "In the highest rank among the mystics of past ages, who have been endowed with signal graces and singular privileges...must be placed, without hesitation, the Venerable Mary of Jesus, called of Agreda...."[4]

Additionally, Maria is one of several past saints whose bodies are considered incorruptible. Her physical body refuses to let the process of decay take over. The flush of her cheeks and other life-like features continue to mystify skeptics. Her body was examined in 1909 and a thorough report was written. Then again in 1989 another examination was performed. The doctor realized there was absolutely no sign of deterioration when compared to the previous medical report written 80 years prior! After more than 320 years, her body is still pristine and unsusceptible to decay.[5]

When we live in the Glory presence of God, our physical bodies begin to take on the life of Christ—even after death. This is just another mystical sign that causes us stop and wonder.

St. Anthony of Padua (1195-1231) is another saint who performed many extraordinary miracles, including bilocation. Once, while he was preaching on Easter Sunday in the Cathedral of Montpellier in front of the clergy and an immense group of people, he remembered he was expected to sing at that very moment in a choir at the Solemn High Mass in a neighboring monastery. Distraught about the whole ordeal, he threw the hood from his cloak over his head and leaned back in the pulpit and was quiet for a long time. His biographer continues:

St. Anthony Of Padua

> At the moment when he ceased speaking in the cathedral, though all the while visible to the congregation, he appeared in the monastery choir among his brethren and sang his office. At the close of the service he recovered himself in the pulpit of the cathedral and, as his chronicler says, finished his sermon with incomparable eloquence.[6]

St. Anthony of Padua was a mult-gifted preacher. He was extremely intelligent, possessed a good speaking and singing voice, and had a great memory. He often moved in miracles and healing, as well as the spirit of prophecy. A few other titles he was given were, "The Hammer of Heretics," because he was an extraordinary polemicist who confidently debated heretics, as well as the "Evangelical Doctor," and "The Wonder-Worker of Padua."

Another interesting account of bilocation is that of **St. John Bosco** (1815-1888), also know as Don Bosco, the founder of the Salesians, an

St. John Bosco

order named in honor of St. Francis de Sales, whom St. John significantly admired. St. John Bosco greatly enjoyed working with children and utilized teaching methods based on love rather than punishment. He is the only Saint to have been given the title, "Father and Teacher of Youth."

One of the saint's most impressive accounts of bilocation is when he was in Turin, Italy, and bilocated to the Salesian College of Sarria in Spain to give instructions to Fr. Branda about

some troubled youths. These young men were plotting a serious crime, all the while pretending to be upright students. This demonstration of bilocation took place in 1886 and happened as follows:

> In the first instance, during the night of January 28-29, Fr. Branda was sound asleep when he heard the voice of Don Bosco calling him by name and instructing him to get up and follow him. Fr. Branda went back to sleep after he decided it must have been a dream, since he knew Don Bosco was in Italy. A week later, during the night of February 5-6, he again heard the voice of Don Bosco and saw him standing at the foot of his bed. Fr. Branda got up quickly, dressed, approached the Saint and kissed his hand as a sign of respect. The Saint then said, "Your house is going on well. I am pleased with you, but there is one dark spot." Suddenly Fr. Branda saw an apparition of

four young men, two of whom he recognized as boarders of the house and two as pupils. With a look of anger and severity, Don Bosco pointed at one of the apparitions and said, "Tell this one to be more prudent. As for the others, they must be expelled. Show them no pity, and do it as soon as possible."

After this took place, St. John Bosco led Fr. Branda back to his room. They passed through two more dormitories. St. John didn't use a key, nor did he need to touch a door handle—the doors simply opened before them as the illuminating halo that surrounded him touched the doors. This heavenly light seemed to brighten the way before them. Just before St. John disappeared, leaving Fr. Branda alone in the dark, he repeated his command to expel the three boys.

Fr. Branda decided to wait to expel the youths because he had no physical evidence or proof of their guilt. Three days later he received a letter in the mail from Fr. Rua which stated: "As I was walking with Don Bosco today under the porticoes of the Oratory he bade me ask you whether you had carried out the order he had himself intimated to you a short time ago."[7]

Waiting still another day, Fr. Branda heard a voice in his spirit while preparing for morning Mass. The voice said that if he failed to carry out the command, this would be his last Mass. Directly after the gathering he did as he was told and promptly expelled the boys. But not until after the boys had unwittingly confessed that they saw the illuminated St. John Bosco by their bedsides a few nights prior![8]

Jeff Jansen of Global Fire Ministries had a similar bilocation experience that was witnessed by over 1200 people in a conference in Cincinnati, Ohio and documented by well-known Christian leaders of our day. Jeff writes:

The Visitation

I had been in a season of pressing hard into the Lord, spending many hours in the presence of God and ascending into the heavens. I've had

Jeff Jansen

many breakthroughs and encounters in the Glory of God, but what was about to happen would change my life and the ministry. I remember after prayer one night, I went to bed early, as I had been working and ministering to make ends meet. Often as I would go to bed, I would extend myself into the throne room and minister to the Lord until I fell asleep. Many times, the Lord would come and sit at the end of my bed and spend time with me. Other times the glory of God would come over the top of my head as a lamp or a ball of light. With my eyes closed and the lights off in the bedroom, the light from the glory of God would be so intense my whole body would shake as waves of Gods love would ripple over me. It was pure ecstasy!

That night I was awakened at 11:22 P.M. by the blast of a trumpet. Two angels with long silver trumpets were standing at the foot of my bed and blowing an alarm in my ears. I now understand what John felt like on the Island of Patmos when he said he felt like a dead man. The fear of the Lord filled my body, and I was completely undone in the hands of God. The angel on my left side blew a trumpet in my left ear. This is what woke me up. The angel on my right was blowing his trumpet in my right ear, only what came out of it was not a sound, but a hot wind that entered my body, went down into my chest, into my spirit man, and exploded in electric power.

Immediately I was pulled out of my body, through the roof, through the atmosphere, and past the stars, and I came to rest in a large room in Heaven called the Room of Intercession. I remember thinking this must be a dream. As I looked around, I saw men, women, children, and angels all praying over the nations. I saw the regions of the earth flash before me in a moment of time. Everything was so surreal; I could scarcely take in what I was seeing. In the experience I looked around and saw myself lying on the floor, yet I was standing above myself at the same time. As I was watching myself, praise began to flow from my spirit man. When you're in Heaven, what is in you comes out. I was saying, "Lord, You are so awesome; Lord, You are so beautiful; Jesus, You are so wonderful, You are so incredible." This praise was coming out of my mouth, only I noticed there were two voices coming out of me. There was my voice and the voice of the Holy Spirit, harmoniously singing and declaring the goodness of the Lord.

Portals of Glory

This encounter lasted through the evening and into the morning. As I awoke my eyes were opened to a whole new dimension in the Spirit. I was prolifically seeing angels, beings, and shafts of light that would move through the house like colorful supernatural pathways reaching from my living room into the heavens.

My spirit man had awakened to a brand new place in the Glory of God. Rainbows would appear in meetings, and clouds of Glory would manifest as I would preach. Miracles would explode in the atmosphere with tangible signs of the Glory. Often fireballs or honey wheels would be released in meetings, and the whole house would be wacked under the power of God. We were seeing gold teeth, gold dust, gemstones, and other wonderful signs with many healings and creative miracles. God had shifted me, shifted the ministry, shifted our lives, and we would never be the same.

One significant event that shocked our family, friends, and well-known leaders happened at a meeting in Cincinnati, Ohio. I was scheduled to be at a conference there called "Engaging the Revelatory Realm of Heaven." The host pastors were friends of mine, as I had ministered at their church often. They had invited me to be with them along with Rick Joyner, James Goll, Patricia King, Paul Keith Davis, and an approximate 1,200 people in attendance. God was moving powerfully in Cincinnati, and there was a heavy expectancy that God was going to do something wonderful.

The conference started on a Thursday night. I wasn't able to attend due to a prearranged event in Nashville. I told the host pastors that I would not be there for the opening sessions on that Thursday night but would drive to Cincinnati early Friday morning and be there for the opening session. I did exactly that. I kept my appointment in Nashville with a group of friends of mine and then returned to our house for fellowship, ending the night with communion, praying for one another, and talking about the Glory of God. Only, something strange happened during the communion service. During communion my body became electric with the fire of God, and I felt like I was expanding and would come apart. I told Jan, "Something is happening to my body....Something is happening to my body, I feel like I'm going to explode!" This experience happened for what seemed like an hour. Then the evening wrapped up, we said goodbye to our guests, and we went to bed around 10:30 P.M.

The Heavenly Visitor

The alarm woke me at 3:00 A.M., and I scampered to pack my bags to get on the road to the meeting in Cincinnati. I drove through the night and pulled up at the church at 8:30 A.M. As I entered the church, the worship was already at full throttle. I walked up to the registration table, filled out my own name badge and put it on, signed my name in the guest book, and entered the sanctuary. Finding my seat in the front I sat down with the other speakers. I was in the sessions all day and through the evening.

At the end of the evening session the host pastors found me and hugged me and said, "Jeff, we're so sorry it's taken this long to get to you. We saw you come in last night but we've been so busy with details of the conference we weren't able to get to you."

I said, "No, actually, I just got here this morning as I drove through the night to get here and have been in the meetings all day, and I'm bushed and am going to the room to go to bed."

They said to me, "Well, actually we saw you last night in the balcony and acknowledged you from the pulpit."

I proceeded to correct them and said, "No, actually, I just got here this morning as I drove through the night and am exhausted, and I'm going to the room so I can catch up on my sleep."

I'll never forget the puzzled look on their faces. They said, "Jeff, what are you talking about? Don't you remember us waving to you in the balcony? You waved back at us as you were ministering to others up there."

At this point the MC of the event, listening to the unfolding of events, said to me, "Jeff, you were here last night. Don't you remember our conversation? Don't you remember laying hands on me and praying for me?" Supposing I didn't remember him, he said, "I'm the guy that filled out your name badge and put it on you. You signed your name in the guest book. Don't you remember?"

I came to find out there were over 50 people that I ministered to, laid hands on, prayed for, and prophesied over in the meeting in Cincinnati on that Thursday night, while at the same time I was in another meeting in Nashville, Tennessee, in the Glory of God. I was flabbergasted as I listened to reports of how I ministered to dozens of people that night. Most of the people were people I personally knew. Many of the words were simple words of encouragement. Others were directives for their lives.

Immediately, the buzz at the conference was, "Did you hear about Jeff Jansen's angel showing up Thursday night?" *My angel?* I thought to myself, *Why was my angel here? God what's going on? Angels don't physically manifest and pray and prophesy over people, do they?*

It seemed I was being questioned by everyone about the details. They all wanted to know exactly what happened. Leaders were calling my wife and inquiring about the meeting in Nashville to confirm that I had actually been there. It was becoming quite clear that something profoundly supernatural had occurred, and we were all wanting to understand what the Lord was doing. What was God saying? Finally, I decided I had had enough and left for home. Still pondering the event, I decided to call Bob Jones. I rang the phone and after the third ring Bob picked up. I said, "Hi Bob, this is Jeff Jansen."

He said, "Oh really? Is this really you, or your angel?"

I said, "Oh man, somebody already called you."

Bob said, "That's right. Now tell me, what do you think happened?"

I said, "I don't know Bob. The whole thing is kind of wild. I think it's like Peter who was locked up in prison, and the angel came and opened up the prison doors and let him out. He went to the place where the others were and knocked on the door. When they opened the door, they said, 'Peter is here.' They said, 'It must be Peter's angel, because Peter is locked up in jail.' I think it's kind of like that. I wanted to be there but wasn't able to."

Bob said, "Nope, that's not it."

A Modern Day Sign and Wonder

Bob said, "They must really trust you to be a prophet there."

I said, "Yes they do."

Bob replied, "Do you realize that sometimes your Older Brother will take the face of a trusted, familiar friend and go on before and tell everything He is getting ready to do in a region? Like He did with the two on the road to Emmaus. They were two of Jesus' disciples, but when Jesus had shown up, it says that they didn't recognize Him because He appeared to them in another form!"

Bob said to me, "You better tell those people in Cincinnati that they better pay close attention to what that man that looked like you said to them."

Bob then proceeded to tell me that things like this used to happen to him in the 1980s. Well, the pastors and leaders wanted this all documented, so we decided to gather all the people the following Sunday and record all of the testimonies in the congregation. There were over 40 people from the region and many more that were not able to be there. I'm still getting reports today of people that were ministered to that Thursday night. Rick Joyner and Paul Keith Davis released an article through the *Morning Star Journal* and other prophetic publications called "Present Day Signs and Wonders."

We are to test everything by its fruit. The fruit of this event overall was positive and encouraging. Many people were amazed that God would love them enough to send a heavenly visitor to speak words of love and encouragement to them.

Who Was "The Man"?

There are two theories as to who "the man" was. As mentioned in the previous sections on bilocation, many saints in the past have had supernatural experiences like this as their lives were given to devotion, contemplative prayer, and communion. I had just been in a deep season of soaking and was having communion in Nashville the night of the encounter. My body felt like it was going to dematerialize, but I never left the room; I never left Nashville! Others who have had bilocation experiences have been aware that they were somewhere else, and some were not aware.

I come from a line of revivalists and wonder-workers called the "Jansenists," who originated from Amsterdam, Holland. They moved in pretty extreme signs and wonders, which could explain things a bit. Years ago the Lord told me I had revivalist blood in my background. I told Him I didn't understand. Within two weeks someone had given me a book by Pat Robertson called *The 100 Years of the Holy Spirit*. In it he attributed the Jansenists as displaying some of the most incredible demonstrations of miracles, signs, and wonders ever recorded.

Another theory, as Bob Jones believes, is that it was in essence Jesus taking the face of a familiar friend and revealing His heart and intentions for an entire region. On any account, something supernatural had occurred. I guess this is why these events are called signs and wonders. They're signs that make us wonder!

The Jansenists

Over the past two thousand years of Christian history, there have been many renewals, revivals, and reforms. For example, among the Monatanists in the second century, the ecstatic utterances of a "new prophecy" brought a sense of excitement and apocalyptic zeal. Among the Jansenists of 17th-century France, Catholic reformers spoke in tongues and prophesied and introduced a new sacrament called the "consolamentum."[9]

Around 1720, the Camisards (French Protestants) spoke in tongues and prophesied in ecstatic trances. In their foretelling, they prophesied the imminent destruction of the Roman Catholic Church in France. Not long after, the Camisards fled to England and America as predecessors of the Shakers.

During this time, the Jansenists moved in and experienced incredible signs, wonders, miracles, healings, and supernatural signs. For years there were documented accounts of supernatural feats being performed among Jansenists.

Cornelius Jansen (1585-1638)

"Jansenism" was founded in the early seventeenth century by Cornelius Jansen, and from the start it was at odds with both the Roman Catholic Church and the French monarchy. Many of the beliefs diverged sharply with standard church doctrine, but it was a popular movement and quickly gained followers among the French populace....As a result, both the church and the king were constantly maneuvering to undermine the movement's power. One obstacle to these maneuverings, and one of the factors that contributed to the movement's popularity, was that Jansenist leaders seemed especially skilled at performing miraculous healings.

One of the most remarkable displays of miraculous events ever recorded took place in Paris in the first half of the eighteenth century. The events centered around a puritanical sect of Dutch-influenced Catholics known as Jansenists, and were precipitated by the death of a saintly and revered Jansenist deacon named Francois de Paris. Although few people living today have even heard of the Jansenist miracles, they were one of the most talked-about events in Europe for the better part of a century.

Cornelius Jansen

It was on May 1, 1727, at the height of this power struggle, that Francois de Paris died and was interred in the parish cemetery of Saint-Medard, Paris.

Because of the Abbe's saintly reputation, worshipers began to gather at his tomb, and from the beginning a host of miraculous healings were reported. The ailments thus cured included cancerous tumors, paralysis, deafness, arthritis, rheumatism, ulcerous sores, persistent fevers, prolonged hemorrhaging, and blindness. But this was not all. The mourners also started to experience strange, involuntary "spasms" or "convulsions" and to undergo the most amazing contortions of their limbs.

These convulsions quickly proved contagious, spreading like a brush fire until the streets were packed with men, women, and children, all twisting, turning, and shaking under the power of the Holy Spirit of God! Shakers and Quakers.[11]

The Spirit of Might

It was while they were in this trancelike state that the Jansenist "Convulsionaires," as they came to be called, displayed the most phenomenal of their talents. One was the ability to endure without harm an almost unimaginable variety of physical tortures. These included severe beatings, blows from both heavy and sharp objects, and strangulation—all with no sign of injury, or even the slightest trace of wounds or bruises.

What makes these miraculous events even more unique is that they were witnessed by literally thousands of observers. The frenzied gatherings around Abbe Paris' tomb were by no means short-lived. The cemetery and the streets surrounding it were crowded day and night for years, and even two decades later miracles were still being reported. To give some idea of the enormity of the phenomena, in 1733 it was noted in the public records that over 3,000 volunteers were needed simply to assist the Jansenist Convulsionaires and make sure, for example, that the female participants did not become immodestly exposed during their convulsions. As a result, the supernatural abilities of the Convulsionaires became an international sight, and thousands flocked to see them, including individuals from all social strata, and officials from every educational, religious, and governmental institution imaginable, witnessed the numerous accounts of both official and unofficial miracles which are recorded in the documents of the time.[12]

Indestructible New Martyrs

It appears nothing could harm these Convulsionaires. They could not be hurt by the blows of metal rods, chains, or timbers. The strongest

of men could not choke them. Some were crucified and afterward showed no trace of wounds. Most mind-boggling of all, they could not even be cut or punctured with knives, swords, or hatchets! Louis-Basile Carre de Montgeron [an investigator, noted authority on the subject, and

Convulsionaires

member of the Paris Parliament] cites an incident in which the sharpened point of an iron drill was held against the stomach of a Convulsionaire and then pounded so violently with a hammer that it seemed "as if it would penetrate through the spine and rupture all the entrails." But it didn't, and the Convulsionaire maintained an "expression of perfect rapture, crying, 'Oh, that does me good brother; strike twice as hard, if you can, next time!'"

> "The spirit of might" was not the only talent the Jansenists displayed during their trances. Many moved in the high level word of wisdom and word of knowledge by the Spirit of revelation and were able to "discern hidden things of the heart."[13]

Lifting off the Ground

Others could read even when their eyes were closed and tightly bandaged, and instances of "lifting up" off of the ground, or as some would say, levitation, were reported. One was so "forcibly lifted up into the air during his Convulsionaire's ecstatic trance that even witnesses tried to hold him down and could not keep him from rising off of the ground."[14]

Invulnerable to Fire

The cases of the Convulsionaires resemble recent revivals, but exceed them in the marvelous and miraculous. Montgeron, however, gives the fullest proofs of their reality, and even Bishop Douglas admits that many of these patients (as they were called) were *invulnerable to fire!*

Many martyrs throughout church history, including St. John, were indestructible. They tried to boil John in oil and he would not die. They tried to cut off his head and he wouldn't die. They finally exiled him to the island of Patmos where he received the book of Revelations. Shadrach, Meshach, and Abednego would not burn either as King Nebuchadnezzar threw them into the fiery furnace for not worshiping his idol. After being seen with the fourth man in the furnace, they came out of the fire unharmed and didn't even have the smell of smoke on their clothes. They were tuned to another frequency! Fire could not touch them![15]

Jansenist Mass Miracles

There surely never was so great a number of miracles ascribed to one person as those which were lately said to have been wrought in France upon the tomb of the Abbe Paris....The curing of the sick, giving hearing to the deaf and sight to the blind, were everywhere talked of as the usual effects of the Jansenists. But, what is more extraordinary, many of the miracles were immediately proved upon the spot, before judges of unquestioned integrity, attested by witnesses of credit and distinction, in a learned age, and on the most eminent theater that is now in the world....Dr. Middleton, in his book *Free Enquiry,* wrote that the evidence of these miracles is fully as strong as that of the wonders recorded of the Apostles. The phenomena so well authenticated by thousands of witnesses before magistrates, and in spite of the Catholic clergy, are among the most wonderful in history.

A Convulsionaire bends back into an arc, her lower back supported by the sharp point of a peg, and a stone weighing fifty pounds, and suspended by a rope passes over a pulley fixed to the ceiling. The stone, being hoisted to its extreme height, falls with all its weight upon the patient's stomach, her back resting all the while on a sharp point of the peg. Montgeron and numerous other witnesses testified to the fact that neither the flesh nor the skin of the back were ever marked in the least, and the girl suffered no pain whatsoever, crying out "strike harder."

Many of these Convulsionaires were weak-framed women who

received tremendous blows to the chest as they would lay on the ground, which in any normal state would have pounded them to a jelly. One Convulsionaire lay upon a stout peg fixed in the ground eight to ten inches high, sharply pointed, with half a dozen persons standing on his chest, but without the peg piercing or hurting him in the slightest.

Montgeron says that Janee Moulu, a girl twenty-two or twenty-three, standing erect, with her back against a wall, received upon her stomach and belly one hundred blows of a hammer, weighing from twenty-nine to thirty pounds, which were administered by a very strong man. Carre de Montgeron himself having given her sixty blows with all his force found it so ineffective, that the hammer was placed in the hands of still a stronger man, who gave her a hundred blows more. In order to test the force of the blows, Montgeron tried them against a stone wall. At the twenty-fifth blow, he says, "the stone upon which I have struck became loose and everything that retained it fell on the other side of the wall, and made an aperture more than half a foot in size."

Upon another Convulsionaire a plank was laid, and as many men got upon it as could stand. Montgeron says he saw a girl likewise pressed under a weight enough to crush an ox. Dr. Bertrand declares these events strange and inconceivable, but too well attested to be disputed. M. de Montegre declares the evidence so complete, and so authentic, as to preclude all rational doubt. Boyer, a contemporary author, says these Convulsionaires could see perfectly with their eyes bandaged.

La Taste, a declared enemy of the Jansenists, declares that he had seen Convulsionaires who discerned and told the thoughts of others, and displayed a supernatural knowledge of things impenetrable to all human perception.[16]

Endnotes

1. Fr. D.F.Miller, C.S.S.R. and Fr. L.X. Aubin, C.S.S.R., *St. Alphonsus Liguori* (Rockford, IL: TAN Books & Publishers, Inc., 1987), 270-271.

2. Rev. Angelo Pastrovicchi, O.M.C., *St. Joseph of Copertino* (St. Louis, MO: B. Herder Book Co., 1918; Rockford, IL: TAN, 1980), 83-84.

3. Joan Carroll Cruz, *Mysteries, Marvels, Miracles* (Rockford, IL: TAN Books and Publishers, Inc., 1997), 31-33.

4. James A. Carrico, *Life of Venerable Mary of Agreda—Author of the Mystical City of God: The Autobiography of the Virgin Mary* (San Bernardino, CA: Crestline Book Company, 1959), 45-50.

5. "María de Agreda," *Wikipedia,* www.en.wikipedia.org/wiki /Maria_de_Agreda (accessed March 24, 2009).

6. Charles Warren Stoddard, *Saint Anthony, The Wonder Worker of Padua* (Rockford, IL: TAN Books & Publishers, Inc., 1971), 56.

7. A. Auffray, S.D.B., *Saint John Bosco* (Tirupattur, South India: Salesian House, 1959), 219.

8. Ibid., 220.

9. Vinson Synan, *The Century of the Holy Spirit* (Nashville, TN: Thomas Nelson Inc., 2001), 15.

10. Ibid., 421.

11. John McManners, *Church and Society in Eighteenth-Century France* (Oxford: Oxford University Press, 1999), 423-454.

12. William Howitt, *The History of the Supernatural in All Ages and Nations and in All Churches* (London: Longman, Roberts and Green, 1863), 130-149.

13. Ibid.

14. Ibid.

15. Ibid.

16. Ibid.

CHAPTER 5

THE NEW GLORY REVIVAL

There are great destiny doors opening to the Church in this season offering new opportunities for spiritual advancement into the supernatural. We have crossed a threshold in God's timeline, and the Glory of God is being revealed with fresh power and new demonstrations of the miraculous. We've had great forerunning mothers and fathers that have imparted much to us, so we must get from them what was imparted. On January 16, 1956, during the height of the great tent revival that swept America and the world, William Branham stood up in the Church of Philadelphia in Chicago, Illinois, and prophesied that "America had turned down her opportunity with the Lord."

Because William Branham was the forerunning prophetic voice of the day, the tent revivals and the move of the Holy Spirit literally stopped at this word. They, too, were given a chance to step into supernatural advancement, but America missed her opportunity. She refused God's offer! The Lord told me in 2006 that He was offering the Church a "Golden Jubilee," as it marked the 50 year anniversary of Branham's word to the Church. This invitation must be understood and apprehended as we pass through the doors of destiny to encounter the Lord in genuine and experiential ways.

A Move of God Must Keep Moving

There are many that have been desperate for the new move of God. God promises to fill those who hunger and thirst for Him, and we're beginning to see the outpouring of our holy desperation. Those who seek the new will find the new. For a move of God to be a move of God, it has to keep moving. The Lord told the children of Israel to follow the cloud by day and the pillar of fire by night. When it moves, you move. Sadly, many have become content with past revivals or moves, and when God begins to move again they are simply satisfied with the level of anointing they have and never move on to the next level.

Bob Jones recently had an encounter with an angel called Breakthrough Revival. The angel appeared to Bob, along with 11 other resurrection angels, and told him many things about the coming Glory revival. He said he had been in the United States for the past few years preparing the way for the greatest revival to ever sweep America. Stadiums will not be big enough to contain the harvest that will come in. The angel shouted three words at Bob: "Move, move, move! You tell the Church we'll be working with those who move in faith." We don't need to have it all figured out, but we need to start moving in faith. In order to get Heaven and the angels to move with us, we must first move. As we've been pressing into the new, God has been meeting us. The Lord told me just recently that I couldn't outrun His Glory Train, and believe me, I've been trying!

New Levels in the Glory

We must rise into the new levels of Glory. I've heard it said that it's a form of insanity to keep doing the same thing over and over again and expect a different result. We must rise up into the new if we are to expect the new!

> *Arise [. . . rise to new life]! Shine (be radiant with the glory of the Lord), for your light has come, and the glory of the Lord has risen upon you* (Isaiah 60:1 AMP).

The Lord promises that if we will get up and begin to move into Him, His glory will rise on us, and we will shine and be radiant with His Glory. *"Then you shall see and be radiant, and your heart shall thrill and tremble with joy. . ."* (Isa. 60:5 AMP). Are you hungry? Do you want to be *thrilled* and *tremble* with joy?

Get Ready

The question to the Church is: Are you hungry for the new? Have you had enough of the status quo? Do you want God no matter how He shows up? Will you not be offended when He comes in a way you haven't expected? Get ready for great increase in the supernatural. Get ready for great explosions of power. Get ready for new levels in the Glory of God like you have never experienced or heard of before. This is the season for it. Jesus said, *"Blessed is he who does not take offense at Me"* (Luke 7:23). I'm telling you now that God is presenting this Glory revival in a way that will attract only the desperate and hungry. The hungry always seem to see what God is doing in the strangest of circumstances because their desire for Jesus causes them to look past the natural to see by the Spirit.

As we move forward, we must judge by one thing and one thing alone—the anointing. First John says, *"But you have an anointing from the Holy One, and you know all things"* (1 John 2:20 NKJV). In this season we must say "Yes!" to the Lord. We will not resist Him again. In this season we must fully embrace and experience the new waves of the Glory of God.

Get ready for the new Glory Revival! Get ready to see whole churches, cities, and regions completely transformed by the Glory of God as the Church rises into her place of authority, releasing new power and new glory and demonstrating the true nature of God evidenced by tangible signs and wonders and wild displays of the Kingdom. The Glory will intensify as believers come together in worship and bask in the awe of God's presence, bringing their love and devotion as a love offering to the Lord of Glory. The multitudes will understand who God is; hundreds, thousands, and even millions will come to the brightness of His shining. Eventually, nations will hear of it and come to behold the Glory of God. I can see hot spots in the United States that will have ongoing Glory revivals that will lead to the restoration of open-air meetings in large fields and tents packed with thousands.

We've seen some pretty remarkable things in the past, but they have all been "previews to the coming attraction." They will all pale in comparison to the outpouring of this new Glory revival. Limbs will grow out and body parts will be recreated right in front of the masses. The tent revivals of the '40s and '50s will dwarf in comparison as raw supernatural power is released on display over and over again. Tangible glory will be evidenced as gold dust, supernatural golden oil, and gemstones appearing, as water turning to wine, and as glory clouds exploding in the atmosphere. We've had these tangible signs appearing in many of our Glory meetings, and we expect them to come with more frequency as the Glory intensifies. I've included photos taken of many of the manifestations of Glory in our meetings.

Past Wonder-Workers

Mystical wonder-workers of the past have revealed to us by their lives what is available to an entire generation. As we've seen in the last two chapters, there have been forerunners throughout history who have crossed over and tasted of the good Word and the power of the Kingdom age (see Heb. 6:4-5). However, that which is coming is not a handful

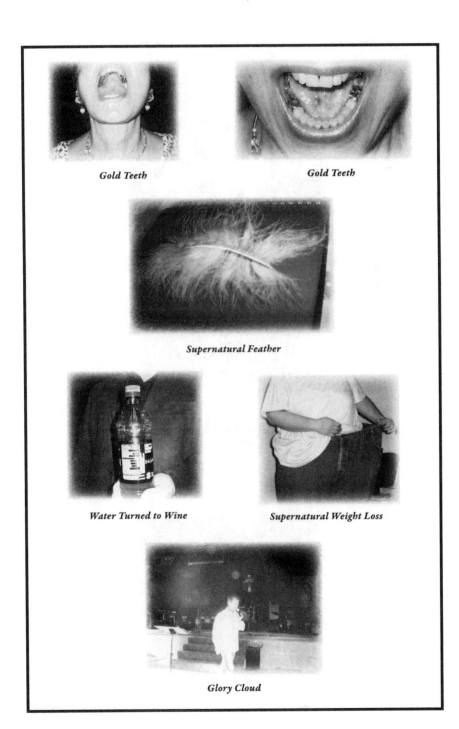

Gold Teeth

Gold Teeth

Supernatural Feather

Water Turned to Wine

Supernatural Weight Loss

Glory Cloud

Honeystone

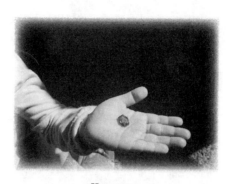

Water into Oil

Gold dust

of wonder-workers, but an entire rising Glory generation of sons and daughters who will beam forth in more radiance than any other generation. They will move in powerful Kingdom dynamics, carrying revival and operating in new dimensions of God's Glory yet to be witnessed. They will be so transformed in their thinking about the power of God that signs, wonders, and miracles will become common occurrences—a natural part of life.

Already we're seeing many operate in powerful dimensions of Christ's authority on earth. This is my prayer and desire for the Body of Christ, and more importantly, it is God's desire for us: that we would release the power of the Spirit of God in us and walk daily in the realms of Glory, spiritually growing in Kingdom dimensions. God is moving and things are shifting as the Holy Spirit moves to bring forth a gloriously transformed Church.

When the Israelites came out of the wilderness, crossed the Jordan River, and entered the Promised Land, they experienced a complete shift and change. Instead of living in His mercy and grace and being sustained by Him with food and provisions, they now had to partner with Him in everything they did. They had to actually *occupy* and *take* the land, which required action on their part. They had to shed one way of thinking for another because the wilderness paradigm no longer applied. God was moving and leading them into the glory of the Promised Land— into His Kingdom to take territory again. It is a drastic change—it's a crossover of thoughts, a transformation of natural thought to spiritual thought, a coming out of an old wineskin and into a new, from a physical realm into a spiritual one.

To operate out of this spiritual dimension is an entirely new dynamic. We have to leave our old way of thinking to see the Kingdom in operation.

Are you ready to be a sign and a wonder that topples the natural earthly order of things and contradicts the laws of physics? Do you want to be a son or a daughter who can command even hurricanes to stop and have them obey? You can, if you walk in the laws of the Spirit.

God is Spirit, and in Him we are spirit beings. A spiritual mindset is vital. We have to shift into the higher law of the Spirit to render the physical law inoperative. When we do, God may just release us as a sign to answer the spiritual hunger of the day, to beam forth Kingdom power and the Glory of the Lord.

In the first few centuries of Christianity, the Holy Spirit moved powerfully in signs, wonders, and miracles through God's people, turning the world upside down (see Acts 17:6). Why are we not doing it today? Why isn't the world running to us? The world is running to the occult for supernatural information. Television and the Internet are full of psychic hotlines, mediums, and wizards because the Church has refused to be the supernatural door of information for the world. The occult offers a dark knowledge of demonic power and allure, with surprisingly accurate information. However, they are climbing up the wrong way to get it and being filled with dark knowledge. This opens them up to demon possession. The Church should be the answer the world is looking for. It is our right and place to do it.

> Behold, I and the children whom the Lord has given me are signs and wonders [that are to take place] in Israel from the Lord of hosts, Who dwells on Mount Zion. And when the people [instead of putting their trust in God] shall say to you, "Consult for direction mediums and wizards who chirp and mutter," should not a people seek and consult their God? Should they consult the dead on behalf of the living?" (Isaiah 8:18-19 AMP)

God has placed it deep within humankind to seek for direction from Him in the realm of the spirit. Because the true children of light aren't providing the avenue for this to happen, the world has abandoned the truth for a counterfeit source. When satan stepped between God and humans in Eden, the flow of communion was severed. They were spiritually cut off from their supernatural source of information, power, and creative ability—abandoned to their own reasoning ability and five senses. Satan had succeeded in blinding humanity from hearing and seeing in the constant state of unbroken fellowship with God in the Glory.

> *For the god of this world has blinded the unbelievers' minds [that they should not discern the truth], preventing them from seeing the illuminating light of the Gospel of the glory of Christ (the Messiah), Who is the Image and Likeness of God"* (2 Corinthians 4:4 AMP).

Satan has blinded people from walking in the knowledge of the Glory of God. He captured humankind's place in dominion as the "god of this world" and became the dictator of the atmosphere, controlling the airwaves as the prince of the power of the air.

> *In which at one time you walked [habitually]. You were following the course and fashion of this world [were under the sway of the tendency of this present age], following the prince of the power of the air. [You were obedient to and under the control of] the [demon] spirit that still constantly works in the sons of disobedience [the careless, the rebellious, and the unbelieving, who go against the purposes of God]* (Ephesians 2:2 AMP)

The spiritual authority that satan obtained in the earth, Adam gave to him.

> *Then the devil took Him up to a high mountain and showed Him all the kingdoms of the habitable world in a moment of time [in the twinkling of an eye]. And he said to Him, "To You I will give all this power and authority and their glory (all their magnificence, excellence, preeminence,*

*dignity, and grace), **for it has been turned over to me,** and I give it to whomever I will"* (Luke 4:5-6 AMP).

Authority was "turned over" to satan by Adam, but Jesus Christ took it and gave it back to believers along with the keys to the Kingdom of Heaven.

> *And I tell you, you are Peter [Greek, Petros—a large piece of rock], and on this rock [Greek, petra—a huge rock like Gibraltar] I will build My church [Jesus speaking of Himself], and the gates of Hades (the powers of the infernal region) shall not overpower it [or be strong to its detriment or hold out against it]. I will give you the keys of the Kingdom of Heaven; and whatever you bind (declare to be improper and unlawful) on earth must be what is already bound in Heaven; and whatever you loose (declare lawful) on earth must be what is already loosed in Heaven* (Matthew 16:18-19 AMP).

Jesus gave back to us the promise of Eden and the mandate of the Garden, which is *complete authority* over the wind, the seas, the animal kingdom, and everything in the earth.

> *Behold! I have given you authority and power to trample upon serpents and scorpions, and [physical and mental strength and ability] over all the power that the enemy [possesses]; and nothing shall in any way harm you* (Luke 10:19 AMP).

This is our heritage and our inheritance. This realm belongs to the glorious Church of Jesus Christ the Messiah. It is the treasure of "Divine Illumination" of the Gospel of the Glory of Christ:

> *For God Who said, "Let light shine out of darkness," has shone in our hearts so as [to beam forth] the Light for the*

illumination of the knowledge of the majesty and glory of God [as it is manifest in the Person and is revealed] in the face of Jesus Christ (the Messiah) (2 Corinthians 4:6 AMP).

The Spirit of Sonship and Glory

Satan is a copier and a liar. When the Church rises in revelation of this, understanding who we are and who He is who lives in us, the world will see the mature Body of Jesus Christ in full operation. Just as Jesus moved on the earth 2,000 years ago, the Church will move as a single Body operating in miracles, healings, signs, and wonders. What He did then, He will do in these last days through a fully mature, corporately anointed Body of believers.

It will be nothing less than Christ in us the hope of Glory, the Creator of the Universe, the third Person of the Godhead who created everything and lives inside each of us. It is nothing less than that divine and holy seed—divine sperm growing us into full maturity. As we enter into this revelation as family—legal sons and daughters—nothing will be impossible for us. As we speak, our words will become *substance* in Glory, and matter will be created. Elements and matter must obey the voices of the members of the family of God—God designed things that way. All things belong to you, all things are yours, you can do all things because hidden treasures of wisdom, knowledge, and revelation *are in* Jesus Christ, and are fully accessible to you.

Transferred into the Dominion of Light

What is your inheritance?

That you may walk (live and conduct yourselves) in a manner worthy of the Lord, fully pleasing to Him and desiring to please Him in all things, bearing fruit in every good work and steadily growing and increasing in and by the knowledge of God [with fuller, deeper, and clearer insight, acquaintance, and recognition] (Colossians 1:10 AMP).

Moreover:

Giving thanks to the Father, Who has qualified and made us fit to share the portion which is the inheritance of the saints (God's holy people) in the Light. [The Father] has delivered and drawn us to Himself out of the control and the dominion of darkness and has transferred us into the Kingdom of the Son of His love (Colossians 1:12-13 AMP).

When you were born, your spiritual father was not God, but the prince of the power of the air. Conceived in sin and born in sin, you were actually born spiritually dead. However, when you became born again, you were translated—the Father delivered and drew you to Himself and away from the control and dominion of darkness. He transferred and shifted you from darkness into the King's domain of light. You could not do it. He carried you over from death into life:

In Whom we have our redemption through His blood, [which means] the forgiveness of our sins. [Now] He is the exact likeness of the unseen God [the visible representation of the invisible]; He is the Firstborn of all creation. For it was in Him that all things were created, in Heaven and on earth, things seen and things unseen, whether thrones, dominions, rulers, or authorities; all things were created and exist through Him [by His service, intervention] and in and for Him (Colossians 1:14-16 AMP).

This is where we're seated—it's who He created us to be. It is our place of ruling with Him as a son or a daughter—a joint heir. Everything belongs to us—all of that belongs to you! God created the invisible realm first and then the heavens and the earth *simultaneously*. The earth is a carbon copy in natural form of the heavens.

> *And He Himself existed before all things, and in Him all things consist (cohere, are held together). He also is the Head of [His] body, the church; seeing He is the Beginning, the Firstborn from among the dead, so that He alone in everything and in every respect might occupy the chief place [stand first and be preeminent]. For it has pleased [the Father] that all the divine fullness (the sum total of the divine perfection, powers, and attributes) should dwell in Him permanently* (Colossians 1:17-19 AMP).

CHAPTER 6

ACCELERATION IN THE GLORY

The Lord showed me recently in an encounter how time is running out and eternity is rushing in. In this experience, I began to understand how, in the Book of Amos, the plowman could overtake the reaper—the eternal realm is literally overtaking time in the natural! As the Body of Christ, we are standing at the threshold of a new era—the brink of a new age. The power for acceleration is in the eternal, timeless realm of the Glory of God. When the realm of Glory moves into the realm of the natural, there comes a great acceleration for miracles, healings, signs, wonders, and the release of creative power. Nearly 2,000 years ago, the author of the book of Hebrews exhorted the Jewish Christians to leave the elementary teachings and principles *about* Christ, urging them to press forward into maturity (see Heb. 6:1). Friends, today I urge you to come before the very throne of God with boldness and confidence—stepping into maturity—as you encounter new realms of the Glory of God.

These are the days when the Glory of God is being revealed in and through the Body of Christ. The Glory of this latter house will be greater than the former (see Hag. 2:9). There is a corporate remnant, an overcoming Body of believers, a rising Glory generation that will rise to new levels of kingly authority and administrate the dominion of the Kingdom of God with great power as it steps into the fullness of the measure of the stature of Christ. This remnant is the *new man* coming forth in the earth. We are about to see the full manifestation of the resurrection power of Jesus as this Body rises to maturity.

In order for us to step into spiritual maturity, I believe it's essential that we first learn how to cultivate an atmosphere of God's presence in our individual lives through devotion, prayer, holiness, and humility. Second, we must learn how to corporately usher in the cloud of Glory through high praise, worship, and faith. And third, in order to step into maturity, we must learn how to operate in and from the realm of Glory. This means receiving revelation by faith through vision and imagination while in the Glory and also speaking and declaring the word of God from the realm of Glory.

Reaping the Seeds of Destiny

The Lord has shown me that we are in this time of acceleration; we have stepped into Amos 9:13—"...*the plowman will overtake the reaper.*" All of eternity is pouring into the present causing us to accelerate forward. Seeds that have been sown in the past—seeds of destiny, both good and evil—are full-grown and ready for reaping. As the realm of eternity is meshed with the present, we are witnessing a culmination of events—loose ends are being tied up before the return of Christ. Things that would normally take ten years to happen will only take ten months—even ten weeks. There is a rapid maturity taking place in the Body of Christ as the cloud of His presence descends and blankets us corporately. This season is not simply coming—it is here.

Right now, through the Glory, God is releasing mandates, mantles, and miracles—the spirits of might and multiplication are being poured out on the believing Body of Christ all over the earth for the purpose of world harvest. In these days we will witness unparalleled demonstrations of the Kingdom of Power and Glory. Additionally, in this time, the Lord is requiring that His people be *set apart* for His plans and purposes—extreme *obedience* and passionate *purity* are essential. Lifestyles of radical *worship* and *faith* are the fuels that will ignite revival fires in this generation—a people wholly consumed with and consecrated in the fiery presence of the living Christ.

The Cloud of Glory and the Anointing

Many don't understand this, but there is a difference between the anointing and the Glory. In the anointing, healings occur, but it's more on an individual level. Through a gift of healing or the working of power, the minister prays for someone and they're healed; then moving to the next, he prays, and they're healed, and so on. The minister is operating in the healing anointing which covers him like a mantle, and he releases it to the people.

The Glory cloud, however, is altogether different. It is like a covering or a canopy that blankets the people—they all get touched. When the cloud of Glory is present, there is direct contact with Heaven—revelation increases, the seer realm is opened, gifts are activated, and miracles happen all over. There are many things being said about the Glory of God, so I want to make sure I define it as clearly as I possibly can. The Glory of God is the manifest Presence and Person of the Lord Jesus Christ. It's that simple. In the presence of God there is limitless abundance for everything we have need of in creative miracles, revelation, and power. The children of Israel were fed, nourished, and protected as a generation in the wilderness in the cloud of Glory, for it was His presence that went with them. This Glory generation and new Glory revival will be marked by one thing and one thing only—the Presence of God.

Creative Power in the Realm of Glory

When God speaks we become impregnated with His words. As time passes, that word grows and develops, eventually causing us to give birth to those specific promises. However, when God's word is spoken in the realm of Glory, the time it takes for the word to grow and mature is reduced to only a few moments—we see the promise instantly. This happens because the realm of Glory is the timeless, eternal realm where God is.

Dr. Renny McLean said,

> God set the earth in time while man was created for the eternal. Man was not designed to die or be sick. Man was made to live in, be filled with, and exist in and out of the Glory of God. The Glory of God is His total manifest presence. Man was created to live in this atmosphere, or Glory of God. Man had the distinction of possessing the DNA of God. He was God-breathed. He was God inspired. He was God's being on the earth. He was ageless, created to live in, and for, eternity even as His Creator in His realm.[1]

The eternal realm is the realm of timelessness.

Healings happen over a period of time. Miracles, however, are instantaneous. It is not hard to believe that God causes our hair and fingernails to grow and our body to go through the natural progression of replenishing and replacing cells—this happens daily. An injury that would normally take weeks or months to be healed will be restored instantly when touched by God's Glory. Time is actually made to serve those who know and understand their rights as citizens of Heaven. When we experience the Glory realm, we are experiencing timelessness.

The realm of Glory also holds creative power. When coming into contact with God's Glory, creative power can be released for creative miracles to take place. A creative miracle is not something broken being fixed, healed, or revived. A creative miracle is when something new is actually created in place of the old. We've seen many creative miracles take place when the Glory cloud manifests: new eyeballs, new eardrums, hearts re-created, legs grown out, etc.

Vision, Imagination, and Faith

There are keys that we need in order to unlock the realm of Glory such as vision, imagination, and faith. It is essential that we begin to see things in the realm of faith and out of the realm of faith. Without faith we can't hear what God is saying. Faith operates from a higher law than the natural laws of matter, space, and time. The person of faith believes and speaks from the eternal realm of the *now*, releasing the unseen realm of Glory into the natural.

The imagination is one of the primary characteristics of the creative side of God. God imagined everything He created before He actually created it. He thought about it first and then spoke it into existence. We too were made in His *image*, but first lived in His *imagination*.

> *Your eyes have seen my unformed substance; and in Your book were all written the days that were ordained for me, when as yet there was not one of them* (Psalm 139:16).

To see into the realm of the supernatural we must be able to envision, imagine, and perceive the realms of Glory through faith, which allows us to become intimately acquainted with Him and His ways.

Worship and High Praises

Many times while ministering in a corporate setting I'll start with praise and worship—this brings the anointing. From there I'll minister under the anointing, seeing healings and miracles. When people begin to praise the Lord and give Him glory for the miracles, the faith level begins to rise. Faith and high praise will usher in the Glory cloud, creating an ideal atmosphere for greater miracles. As the people's expectation increases, so does the Glory.

We must learn to cooperate in forming the cloud of Glory by participating with all of our being—dancing, shouting, and singing with all of our hearts releases the Glory and the Kingdom of God within us and mixes with the Glory in the atmosphere. When we do this, we are partnering with Heaven to create the Glory cloud. Praise higher. Worship Him with all your might like David did. Your worship will create the cloud of His presence, and then He will come in all of His Glory.

Press into the New

Many will not accept this new cloud of Glory. They will evaluate it and give their stamp of disapproval; they will discourage others from diverting to this type of unrestrained worship. We will need to make decisions about where we want to go. Are we hungry for God? Will we pursue Him no matter how it looks or what it costs? When Jesus came to earth and performed miracles, signs, and wonders, He said, *"Blessed is he who does not take offense at Me"* (Luke 7:23).

I don't care how the cloud of His presence comes or what it looks like, as long as He keeps coming. We must be willing to loose our grasp of the old and reach out for the new. The Glory is altogether new. People tend to be comfortable talking about the anointing; the manifest realm of Glory, however, is new terrain that the corporate Body of Christ is beginning to trek into. God is offering this rising Glory generation new dimensions of Glory—we're going to touch places no generation before us has gone.

We were birthed from this realm of Glory, and it's where we should feel the most comfortable—the most fulfilled. Moreover, when we worship God and give Him praise, we are fulfilling our very purpose— our destiny. In this place of Glory, your past sees your future and realizes that it can't go where you are heading—it loses its grip on you. When we step into the Glory, we are experiencing the future; we taste the eternal—and our past simply falls away.

As we step into the cloud of Glory, we are stepping into the realm of *all things are possible*. We cannot go to a worship service thinking God is going to do something new while we hang onto the old—it doesn't work that way. We need to worship God in the *now* and minister to Him in the *new*. We need fresh expectation—fresh faith. God is demanding that we operate by His principles. We must align ourselves with this new move and let go of the old.

We mustn't allow old schools of thought and religious tradition to hold us back from the renewed mindset of this Glory generation. This new paradigm shift is being brought forth and backed up by the revelation and manifestation of the Glory of God by the Holy Spirit. This will not come about in a conventional manner, but rather by a corporate Body of believers who are connected to the Head of the Body, which is Christ. Each person is a living stone that will make up a beautiful spiritual house, with Jesus Christ Himself being the chief cornerstone (see 1 Peter 2:5; Eph. 2:20-22).

The Spirit Language of Heaven

We have access to God by faith. Faith is a higher law than the natural laws. By faith we can bypass space and time, stepping into the timeless realm. Faith is the door between the natural and supernatural dimensions. Without faith we can't enter the spiritual realm; without faith we can't even please God (see Heb. 11:6). It is essential that our faith level rises.

Faith operates from the Spirit of Revelation. When we believe and decree by faith, we are reaching out of the natural realm of limited matter into the spiritual realm of unlimited creative resources. Faith is the language that moves the realm of Glory. The natural man doesn't understand this language, nor can he (see 1 Cor. 2:14). The fallen mind of man doesn't know or understand that he is living below his created potential.

After the fall, God gave man faith to lift him so he could see into the unseen realm and have hope. When Adam fell, he was banished from the realm of Glory and unable to see the place from which he came. But God in His love gave him faith so he could see and have hope of returning there. Without faith, he would have died. Likewise, we access our home of Glory as we pull on it by faith. The faith realm supersedes the lower realm. We must get high in order to have authority over the low. God is calling this Glory generation to go higher than we've ever been before.

> *Now Faith is the assurance (the confirmation, the title deed) of the things [we] hope for, being the proof of things [we] do not see and the conviction of their reality [faith perceiving as real fact what is not revealed to the senses]* (Hebrews 11:1 AMP).

Notice the word that this verse begins with: *now*. When the Glory cloud appears, by faith we have the authority to decree "Now!" And the substance from the supernatural realm will manifest and materialize in the natural. For this to happen, we must know God by revelation, which ignites the faith to produce the substance of a miracle.

The nature of God is faith, so without faith it's impossible to please God. Faith must become who we are, or God's Glory can not abide with us. When we fall back on our fallen Adamic nature, we cut ourselves off from our Life Source. Sin weakens faith, and when we are unrepentant of it, our faith will eventually cease to operate completely. Scripture says that God will beautify the humble (see Ps. 149:4 AMP). When we humble ourselves we are able to step into the place from which we fell and operate from that glorious realm.

Miracles are of this higher dimension and are not influenced by time. Faith is a higher law that exists out of time and operates from the law of higher truth not based on fact. The *truth* is by His stripes you are healed (see 1 Pet. 2:24), but the *fact* is you're sick. Which is dominant, truth or fact? Because truth is from the higher realm of God's presence and promise, it exceedingly triumphs over fact, human intellect, and reasoning—you are healed!

Faith is like a tuner in a radio. A tuner picks up the radio waves in the atmosphere and releases them as sound in the natural. When we tune in to the frequency of Heaven by faith, we can pull back through time and space the new sounds and matter from the realm of the Kingdom. We are radios that are able to speak and decree the sounds of Heaven on earth.

> *I will give you the keys of the Kingdom of Heaven; and whatever you bind (declare to be improper and unlawful) on earth must be what is already bound in Heaven; and whatever you loose (declare lawful) on earth must be what is already loosed in Heaven* (Matthew 16:19 AMP).

Supernatural matter will only be loosed on the earth in the faith realm if it is already loosed in the Glory realm. It is necessary for us to understand the nature and ways of God as well as the spiritual Kingdom laws that govern the universe if we want to operate in the supernatural.

New Faith Realms

The Church is about to enter a new realm of faith where we are going to see an increase in the miraculous. In this place of faith there will be opportunity for us to learn how to operate in the realm of Glory. In order for us to do this, it's first necessary that we understand a little bit about the realm of the spirit in correlation with the natural realm. The physical world was created and birthed from the spiritual realm. Everything in the natural was birthed from a realm we cannot detect with our natural senses. Like we talked about earlier, the natural man cannot receive the things of the spirit—therefore, it's our spirits that are able to sense, recognize, and experience the spiritual realm. It's your spirit that receives revelation from the spirit realm. Supernatural substance is constantly being released between these two realms—both the natural and the spiritual.

The reason we don't see more supernatural flow manifesting from Heaven is because we aren't discerning what God is releasing. If we have our senses opened, we will be able to see what is coming from the realm of Glory. We can take what we see and decree it—this will frame it in time, and it will manifest in the natural. The dilemma that people often run into is that by the time they see into the realm of Glory and act on it, the window of opportunity has closed. Then they have to open it up again through praise and thanksgiving.

As we worship we are creating the cloud of Glory. As we praise God the atmosphere will thicken and become spiritually heavy. It is here, when the spiritual climate is right, that we can speak into the cloud of Glory and see a release of miracles.

There are both physical and spiritual requirements for releasing the miraculous. If we don't speak, nothing will happen. If the cloud isn't present, nothing will happen. We need the cloud of Glory present, and we need to speak into it. It is time for us to switch gears and begin to operate in spiritual understanding and revelation.

In the natural world we learn by gathering information with our five senses. In the spirit realm we gain revelation with our spiritual senses. Revelation is nothing more than the revealed mechanics of God that enables us to think and operate from the supernatural dimension. We must stop questioning God. Instead of always looking for logical answers to natural problems, why don't we respond to God in faith? As we do, we will ascend into higher levels of Glory and see a greater manifestation of the miraculous.

Faith to Release Creative Miracles

Then the Lord said to Moses, "See, I make you as God to Pharaoh. . . . (Exodus 7:1).

This is an hour when the Lord is manifesting His Glory upon the earth. He is calling us to a place of radical faith—faith that releases the miraculous. He is pouring on the Church the same anointing for miracles that was upon both Moses and Elijah. God desires that your eyes would be opened to see Him as "Creator God" and that you would see yourself in the likeness of God and grasp the reality for miracles flowing through your life. We need to understand the difference between healings and creative miracles, discover the power contained in the spoken word, and receive keys for cultivating faith for the supernatural.

God Is Creator

Throughout the years and through our travels around the world, we've witnessed countless healings and creative miracles in conferences and crusades. Psoriasis skin conditions instantly cleared up, dead eyeballs scheduled to be surgically removed restored completely, supernatural weight loss of 40 pounds or more, eardrums that were surgically removed put back in, and gold fillings and crowns supernaturally appear. These are creative miracles that occur in the realm of the Glory of God. In order to experience creative power, it's important that we begin to see God as a "Creator God."

> *In the beginning God created the heavens and the earth* (Genesis 1:1).

In the passage above, the Hebrew word for "God" is *Elohim*. It is critical that we have a revelation of the power of Creator God. Jesus wanted His disciples to understand that He was the Word of power— He was Creator God. As they were on their way across the sea, look how Jesus reveals this to His disciples:

> *And a great windstorm arose, and the waves beat into the boat, so that it was already filling. But He was in the*

stern, asleep on a pillow. And they awoke Him and said to Him, "Teacher, do You not care that we are perishing?" Then He arose and rebuked the wind, and said to the sea, "Peace, be still!" And the wind ceased and there was a great calm (Mark 4:37-39 NKJV).

The disciples were amazed that even the wind and the sea obeyed Jesus. However, if they had possessed a revelation of God as Elohim, Creator, they would have rebuked the wind and spoken to the sea themselves.

When we see God as Creator, we can get the faith we need for creative miracles. We see that, as children of God, made in His image, creative miracles and healings should be normal occurrences for we have His creative nature in us.

The realm of Glory is the manifested presence of God. Out of this atmosphere, the supernatural is released. When God's Glory is present in the room, His creative nature is also. In this atmosphere is the realm of "all things are possible." It is the nature of the Holy Spirit to create; we see Him at work in the beginning:

The earth was formless and void, and darkness was over the surface of the deep, and the Spirit of God was moving over the surface of the waters (Genesis 1:2).

When the Holy Spirit begins to brood and move over us, creative substance is available to be called forth and manifested.

You send forth Your Spirit, they are created; and You renew the face of the ground (Psalm 104:30).

It is the work of the Person of the Holy Spirit that makes creative miracles and healings possible.

Healings Versus Creative Miracles

There is a difference between healings and creative miracles. According to Mark, one of the signs that follows believers is that *"...they will lay hands on the sick, and they* [the sick] *will recover"* (Mark 16:18). Recovery is the process of getting better over a period of time; it's not instantaneous or miraculous.

Miracles, on the other hand, are instantaneous. Once in a meeting, the Holy Spirit was moving over the congregation, and I called out, "God is healing multiple sclerosis!" A 10-year-old boy with multiple sclerosis, whose body on one side was eight inches longer than the other, stood up from his chair. He stepped out in faith, into the Glory—he was instantly made whole. His mother later testified that she could hear the bones crack in his body as he stepped out to respond to the word. The boy was completely restored. This is a great example of the miraculous power that can be released through us.

Creative Power Dwells in Us

When we are born again, we receive with the Spirit of God all of the DNA and genetics that He is. The God who created the seen and unseen worlds dwells inside of us—this is a mystery of beauty. The Godhead, the fullness of Deity, makes His home inside our hearts. Paul says that we should not behave as mere men (see 1 Cor. 3:3). This is because we are far from being merely human—we are possessed by Creator God.

Think about another statement of Paul's:

> *...the Spirit of Him who raised Jesus from the dead dwells in you* (Romans 8:11).

What type of human beings does this really make us? Creative miracles are as easy as Romans 8:11. With this single revelation exploding on the inside of me, I can release faith for creative miracles. The same Spirit that raised Jesus from the dead lives in my belly. Out of faith, as I begin to loose the river of life inside me when the Holy Spirit is present in an atmosphere of Glory, creative miracles will happen. They will manifest. They will explode in my spirit, be released through my mouth, and create and recreate substance from the realm of Glory. *It will happen!* And it's all done by speaking words of faith.

The Power of Spoken Words

> *Death and life are in the power of the tongue . . .* (Proverbs 18:21).

"In the beginning was the Word, and the Word was with God, and the Word was God" (John 1:1). Jesus, as the Word, created all things. In this passage, the Greek word for "Word" is *logos*. Logos can also be interpreted into the English word *matter*. So we can say: "In the beginning was the 'Matter,' and the 'Matter' was with God, and the 'Matter' was God!"

The spoken Word is Matter that creates substance. Therefore, we can see that words spoken in a faith decree come out as energized matter that materializes in the natural realm. As we speak faith decrees when the Glory is thick in the room, spontaneously creative matter appears.

A Frequency Spoken by Jesus

When God spoke the worlds into being, all the frequencies of His Glory became manifest; the universe came into being. A ministry friend of mine, David Van Koevering, who helped in creating the Moog synthesizer and is a well-known physics and revelatory teacher, says:

> From the tiniest vibrating superstring that is causing or singing the atoms that make up the table of 103 elements,

all the way through everything the Hubble telescope sees, are the vibrating frequencies of Jesus' voice.[2]

For by Him all things were created, both in the heavens and on earth, visible and invisible, whether thrones or dominions or rulers or authorities...He is before all things, and in Him all things hold together (Colossians 1:16-17).

The phrase *"He is before all things"* means that He is outside of our time. Jesus said to John the Revelator that He was and is the Alpha (beginning) and Omega (ending). Jesus is outside our concept of time in His eternal now and is causing all things to be.

All Matter Has Memory

When we understand by the spoken Word that we are being re-created in Christ now by His singing our song frequency, our intimacy with Him will change. His song of creation was not something He did 16 billion years ago. He is causing you to be now.

Hebrews 11:1 says that faith is substance. It is the invisible substance from which your physical world was and is being created by Jesus Christ. In her small but powerful book *Quantum Faith,* Annette Capps wrote, "God used faith-substance and word-energy to create the universe. He spoke and the vibration (sound) of His words released the substance that became the stars and planets."[3] When we understand that matter has memory and that every good or evil action, word, or thought is recorded, it is our responsibility to remove, purge, and release evil memory.

Matter has memory, and you can change everything that has been recorded by what you speak and observe, by the words you declare, or by the curses you remove and release in the name of Jesus. You can create protected places by anointing with oil and speaking blessings with your words of faith.

By faith we understand that the worlds were prepared by the word of God, so that what is seen was not made out of things which are visible (Hebrews 11:3).

The worlds were framed by God's *Word*—the seen being brought into existence from the unseen. Likewise, we can call matter from the unseen realm into the visible realm.

*You have heard [these things foretold], now you see this fulfillment. And will you not bear witness to it? I show you specified new things from this time forth, even hidden things [kept in reserve] which you have not known. They are created **now** [called into being by the **prophetic word**], and not long ago; and before today you have never heard of them, lest you should say, Behold, I knew them* (Isaiah 48:6-7 AMP).

By our spoken words we can decree a thing and it will come to pass.

Once I was ministering with Bob Jones and Ryan Wyatt in Cleveland, Ohio. It was Sunday morning, and we had just completed a conference. Bob told me, "We've already given them the meat...just go and give them the dessert!" I decided to preach on the authoritative sons of the Kingdom of God. I explained how all of creation was looking for the manifested sons to step into their rightful place as heirs of all things.

As I was preaching, it was obvious that people weren't listening and were waiting for me to finish. I got irritated at what was happening and felt this indignation blanket me. Right in the middle of my preaching, I yelled out, "And to prove that what I am saying is accurate and that this is a word from God, the wind is going to start blowing at 65 miles per hour and will keep on blowing as a sign that God has given power and authority to His sons over creation and we are to exercise dominion over the earth!"

It was a sunny morning, but within 30 minutes the temperature dropped to below freezing and a north wind began blowing off of Lake Michigan. Eventually the streets were covered with snow, and due to the high volume of wind sheer, the airport was shutdown. We were scheduled to fly out that afternoon. The only thing Bob Jones could say was, "I told you, before you ever give a word like that you should say, '...and this word will take place after I leave the city.' Now look at what you have done!" He was sincerely ticked off. After being stranded at the airport for many hours, they finally cleared us to take off.

Bob called me the next day and said, "Well, you missed it—the front page of the Cleveland paper stated that the wind came in at 64 miles an hour."

Immediately, I came back with, "No Bob, I think they need to recalibrate their wind machines!"

Bob laughed and said, "That was awesome what you did; I think they got the point."

Partnering with God

God wants us to participate with Him in releasing creative miracles. We see this example in Matthew 14 with the feeding of the 5,000. Jesus took the five loaves of bread and the two fish and broke them into pieces, distributing them to His disciples. The disciples then distributed the food among the crowd. Jesus taught them how easy and natural it was for this to happen. As they took one loaf and gave it away, there was always another.

> ... God, who gives life to the dead and calls those things which do not exist as though they did... (Romans 4:17 NKJV).

God calls those things that do not exist into existence. However, it's not that those things didn't exist—they always existed in God. Before time began, in the heart of God, in His very core, those things did exist. He gave birth to them through His spoken word. In this hour, the Lord is calling us to draw near to His heart so we can release His heart. He is pouring out His Spirit upon His sons and daughters and releasing an end-time anointing to bring in the harvest. It is time for us to take dominion over the earth, exercising the power of the spoken word to manifest His Kingdom through creative miracles.

Releasing the New Song

I've often been in meetings where the songs that are being sung have long outlived their day. Don't get me wrong, at one time they had power and carried revelation and a weighty anointing, but they've become familiar and stale. In these services rarely will there be a fresh release from Heaven because the atmosphere that's being created is not filled with faith, passion, and fresh revelation. People just get stuck in song mode.

Our worship is the key to bringing the new sounds and realms of Glory into the earth. It is the song of the Lord that flows from His heart through ours. As we worship, we usher in streams of Heaven that change the atmosphere in which we live. As we join together and our worship intensifies, it will lift us into another realm—the Glory realm.

The new sound that is being released is the sound of His voice riding on the praises of His people. God sings His song through us, releasing the sound of Heaven on earth. The angels listen for the new sound; when they hear it, they come from other nations just to worship. All of Heaven and earth long to worship and see what God may reveal next. Anyone can worship, but not everyone will worship with the new song of God. Until we sing the new song, the greater realm of the Spirit will not be released in our midst.

There is a song in our spirits that can take us to new places in the Glory realm. Nobody can do it for us; we need to do it ourselves. When we release the song that lies dormant in our spirits, it will lift into a greater Glory of His presence.

The *new* song is the *now* song. It is the *prophetic word of the Lord* song that must be sung. The angels search for the aroma that is released from the new song, drawing them like bees to a flower. When they come, they begin to stir the atmosphere of Glory and help release the miraculous. The devil, however, hates when we step over into the new song. He is powerless against it and is locked out of the Glory as the high praises are released.

I've been in worship services where the cloud becomes so thick that a golden hue begins to form in the atmosphere. I've even been privileged to capture the Glory cloud on video. I've seen many photos, but rarely have I seen the cloud on film. When God's people hold back their praises, it doesn't seed the heavens for the much-needed Glory rain.

Many people get caught in asking God to rend the heavens and come down. They cry and call out to God for a visitation when all the while God is saying, "You come up here!" The heavens are open—Jesus has already cleared the way for us to access the Father. "You come to Me!" Our praises rise like incense to the Lord drawing Him to us. Our praise goes up and the Glory comes down.

As we sing the new song, God releases His Word, which brings the framework of Heaven into the now. This is why spontaneous supernatural explosions of Glory manifest when His presence is in the room. The superior realm of Heaven literally collides with the inferior, natural realm of earth, causing the inferior dimension to be instantly affected and changed. Anything that is inferior in the presence of God will be changed. This is why it's mandatory that we change the way we worship. We need to learn what brings Heaven—the old ways just won't cut it. Only the high praises of God will release the new dimensions we long for.

Our Commission

When we are in the cloud of Glory, we are able to declare the word of the Lord and see it supernaturally manifest. We have stepped into Job 22:28: *"You will also decree a thing, and it will be established for you."*

God has given us access to the storehouses of Heaven—provision, miracles, gifts, mantles, blessings, favor, you name it. As we encounter new realms of the Glory in this season, we will see a swift manifestation of the words we speak. Now is the time for us to decree a thing—it will be established.

We are being commissioned by the Lord to step into new realms of Glory through worship and high praise. As we do this together, we are going to see the Kingdom of Power and Glory made manifest. God's Kingdom is taking dominion upon the earth and is displacing every stronghold of the enemy.

> *Let the high praises of God be in their throats and a two-edged sword in their hands...* (Psalm 149:6 AMP).

> *For He must reign until He has put all His enemies under His feet* (1 Corinthians 15:25).

Through high praise we destroy the plans of the enemy and bring to earth new realms of Glory not yet revealed. We are stepping into a realm of timelessness where the miracles in His presence are being made known to us in almost unimaginable ways. As we continue heavenward, we are breaking the constraints of the natural realm and shaking off old paradigms. The doors of Heaven are opening wider than we've ever seen before, and we are witnessing the unfolding of the scrolls of destiny. Both the seen and unseen worlds are being changed from one degree of Glory to another by the ever-increasing Glory of God.

Endnotes

1. Renny McLean, *Eternity Invading Time* (Altamonte Springs, FL: Advantage Books, 2005), 24.

2. David Van Koevering, "The Physics of Worship" (Arkansas City, KS: March 17, 2008).

3. Annette Capps, *Quantum Faith* (England, AR: Capps Publishing, 2003), 22.

[CHAPTER 7]

SOUND, LIGHT, AND THE POWER OF PRAISE

Thanksgiving is key for releasing the Glory of God in our midst. We've seen the most incredible miracles in Glory gatherings, conferences, and meetings around the world by creating an atmosphere of thanksgiving and praise. Supernatural weight loss, blind healed, deaf hearing, crippled walking, and diseases of all sorts are healed in a higher Glory of God that manifests through the power of thanksgiving and praise. Manifestations of Glory flow in abundance in an atmosphere supercharged with praise. There are just a few select places in Scripture where it tells us how to know what the perfect will of God is for your life.

Jesus taught us to pray this way:

> *Your Kingdom come Your will be done, on earth as it is in Heaven* (Matthew 6:10).

The will of God is to make earth look like Heaven. Paul instructed the church in Thessalonica:

In everything give thanks; for this is God's will for you in Christ Jesus (1 Thessalonians 5:18).

The will of God for your life is that you give thanks for everything. Thanksgiving releases the Glory of God and the angels to work on your behalf.

Because the breath of God is in us, we become His voice in the earth. As we speak, He speaks, and His voice is the voice of resurrection power. It is important for us to understand that attitudes shift our spiritual surroundings. Love, joy, peace, hate, jealousy, anger, and self-pity are not just attitudes; there are spirit and power in the emotions that harmonize the spirit and physical realms and generate substance. These attitudes are light that radiate out from us as a force with spiritual impact or vibration for both good and evil.

When God created the worlds, His voice was a vibration that formed the seen realm. These tiny atoms spin at their own intervals according to their own individual vibration or pattern. When Adam sinned, it wreaked such havoc in the physical world that the atoms were literally thrown out of whack, opening the door to demonic vibration from the kingdom of darkness. These demonic vibrations, in turn, brought sickness and disease into the habitable world, but the voice of God is still speaking. We can recreate the physical realm by framing it with the voice of faith.

The Power of Thanksgiving

Science confirms that every created thing is made up of sound waves that are constantly spinning at different intervals, forming objects in matter of various densities both small and great. We also understand sound as a power that, when cranked up to a certain level or frequency, will crush glass or break windows in a house. All sound and color and images are wave lengths that move by vibration and are a power that have substance.

That being said, we need to understand that every attitude carries its own power and vibration that is recognizable in the realm of the spirit. It is not just an attitude—it is a force. This light force of vibration wraps itself around a person as if it were a coat or a jacket that continually pulls a person deeper into itself until they are completely taken over by it, whether for good or bad. Every attitude we release is filled with powerful vibrations wrapping themselves around us like a garment, further enveloping us into its cocoon-like power.

> *For by your words you will be justified and acquitted [set free], and by your words you will be condemned and sentenced [enslaved]* (Matthew 12:37 AMP).

Jesus was saying that the words we wrap ourselves in will either set us free or imprison us here in this life and in eternity to come.

> *Death and life are in the power of the tongue, and they who indulge in it shall eat the fruit of it [for death or life]* (Proverbs 18:21 AMP).

There are spiritual repercussions to the words we release—both good and evil.

> *Your eye is the lamp of your body; when your eye (your conscience) is sound and fulfilling its office, your whole body is full of light; but when it is not sound and is not fulfilling its office, your body is full of darkness* (Luke 11:34 AMP).

The individual that wraps himself in self-pity allows himself to be imprisoned by the power or force of that cloak of darkness. Neville Johnson says that, "Every kind of evil carries its own dark color or 'dark light' and force." Jesus then goes on to say, "Then watch out that the light in you is not darkness" (Luke 11:35).

Jesus referred to this kind of light as "dark light." Every good or evil trait is not only a power, but it carries its own heavenly or demonic "tone" that is destructive or life-giving in nature. Depression carries with it a light that surrounds a person and is discernible in the realm of the spirit. Love, joy, and thanksgiving also have their own color and light with them that attract the angelic realm from the Kingdom of light.

If we can learn to recognize these truths and get the understanding of it, we can change our circumstances by putting off the old nature with its attitudes, cravings, lusts, and appetites and by choice put on the Lord Jesus Christ and the new heavenly nature of love, joy, and peace, which is born from above. By doing this we can break the power and magnetic attraction of demonic darkness and attract Heaven and the angelic realm of light.

The Garment of Praise

Isaiah prophesied to a generation that was yet to come. He said to put on the garment of praise for the spirit of heaviness:

> To grant [consolation and joy] to those who mourn in Zion—to give them an ornament (a garland or diadem) of beauty instead of ashes, the oil of joy instead of mourning, the garment [expressive] of praise instead of a heavy, burdened, and failing spirit... (Isaiah 61:3 AMP).

The Hebrew word for "garment" here is a *mattah*, which means to "wrap oneself in or to veil oneself". When we choose to put on the garment of praise we begin to wrap ourselves in the power and light of that garment, which destroys the spirit of heaviness.

The Hebrew word for "praise" is *hallal*, which means to "*shine forth* with *sound* and *color*." When we begin to praise, we shine with *light* and *color*. So when we choose to praise we wrap ourselves in a supernatural heavenly garment of power and light that flows with an unstoppable force that destroys the spirit of heaviness. When we choose to be thankful we are filled with light, and we put off the power of sadness and despair and dismantle the realm of the demonic.

With our attitudes we are constantly attracting one of two kingdoms—either the Kingdom of light or the kingdom of darkness. All too often we are looking for some kind of super-spiritual answer or remedy to deliver us from our condition, when all we need to do is simply worship and praise our way through it. Our greatest weapons are worship and thanksgiving. Next we will look at what David wrote about praise.

The High Praises of God

> ***Praise*** *the Lord! Sing to the Lord a new song,* ***praise*** *Him in the assembly of His saints! Let Israel rejoice in Him, their Maker; let Zion's children triumph and be joyful in their King! Let them* ***praise*** *His name in chorus and choir and with the [single or group] dance; let them sing praises to Him with the tambourine and lyre! For the Lord takes pleasure in His people; He will beautify the humble with salvation and adorn the wretched with victory. Let the saints be joyful in the glory and beauty [which God confers upon them]; let them sing for joy upon their beds. Let the **high praises** of God be in their throats and a two-edged sword in their hands, to wreak vengeance upon the nations and chastisement upon the peoples, to bind their kings with chains, and their nobles with fetters of iron, to execute upon them the judgment written. He [the Lord] is the honor of all His saints.* ***Praise the Lord!*** *(Hallelujah!) (Psalm 149:1-9 AMP).*

Praise will bind the kings with chains and nobles with fetters of iron. Who are the kings and nobles David was talking about? Both the

natural and demonic kings of Heaven and earth. When the high praises
of God are in our mouths, the two-edged sword is automatically in our
hands, wreaking vengeance upon all of our enemies. Sickness, disease,
depression, oppression, cancer, and every enemy against God's people
will flee in the presence of a praising, thankful people. Satan can't stand
the Glory of God. Every time the Glory of God shows up, he is looking
for the back door. The devil is defeated every time. Praise and thanksgiving have always been the weapons of choice for God's people. For the
Lord is the honor of all His saints. Hallelujah!

Let's look at some other Scriptures that shed light on the power of
praise and thanksgiving.

> For the weapons of our warfare are not physical [weapons
> of flesh and blood], but they are mighty before God for
> the overthrow and destruction of strongholds. [Inasmuch
> as we] refute arguments and theories and reasonings and
> every proud and lofty thing that sets itself up against
> the [true] knowledge of God; and we lead every thought
> and purpose away captive into the obedience of Christ
> (2 Corinthians 10:4-5 AMP)

By putting on the clothing of light and power in thanksgiving and
praise we are able to destroy and overthrow wrong mindsets and negative thinking that keeps us bound in our present condition and circumstances. We are told to praise and thank God in every situation,
regardless of how difficult it is, because it's God's will for us.

> In everything give thanks; for this is God's will for you in
> Christ Jesus (1 Thessalonians 5:18).

Unless we get this understanding, we cannot go any further in God.
We will be held captive and unable to break through the veil of darkness
to get into the realm of light where God wants us to be. When we are

manifesting thanksgiving and praise, it releases a power that will transform us and heal us body, soul, and spirit.

> *Enter His gates with thanksgiving and His courts with praise* (Psalm 100:4).

> *Let the peace of Christ rule in your hearts, to which indeed you were called in one body; and be thankful* (Colossians 3:15).

> *I will praise the name of God with a song and magnify Him with thanksgiving* (Psalm 69:30).

Attracting Heaven

When we manifest faith we are emitting a power and a brilliance that will attract Heaven. Praise is a glorious golden light that manifests in the realm of the spirit. Often we see gold dust and golden oil come in this type of environment. Thanksgiving is this kind of power and glory. When we are thankful it opens up the gates of Heaven for everything we have need of. When we moan and grumble about things in our lives, it attracts a demonic power that will cut us off from Heaven and eventually will even affect the cells in our bodies and the marrow in our bones.

> *A joyful heart is good medicine* (Proverbs 17:22).

Sickness is a vibration that works against the body and causes it to decompose. Faith and thanksgiving are powerful vibrations that destroy sickness when exercised. When we choose to be thankful, a heavenly glorious light and power will fill us and transform us right down to the cells in our body. If we are always talking about sickness, we'll be surrounded by the vibration and demonic power of that sickness. We need to stop

129

talking about sickness. You may feel sick, but stop energizing the sickness by talking about it. Thank God for all the good things in your life and forget sickness and it will die. Depression and self-pity attract a dark presence that will cut you off from the light of the Glory of God and destroy you. Give thanks to God in everything and in every situation, and watch your circumstances instantly change. Watch your body gain new strength and power.

> ...*giving thanks to the Father, who has qualified us to share in the inheritance of the saints in Light* (Colossians 1:12).

> ...*God is Light, and in Him there is no darkness at all* (1 John 1:5).

> *He* [God] *wraps himself in light as with a garment...* (Psalm 104:2 NIV).

> *[The Father] has delivered and drawn us to Himself out of the control and the dominion of darkness and has transferred us into the Kingdom of the Son of His love [the Kingdom of Light]...* (Colossians 1:13 AMP).

What Are We Manifesting?

When we begin to praise God, we immediately become surrounded with heavenly light and the Glory. The spirit world knows who we are not just by our words, but by the color of light that emanates from us. The New Age community calls it an "aura," but the light they see on us is the light of the Glory of God. Demons and angels need only take one good look at us and know immediately who we are by the light coming from us. These attitudes are a power that pours from us and opens up gates that will take us deeper into the emotion and the spirit of an attitude, good or bad. It is clearly, then, our responsibility in everything to overcome with a right attitude and a thankful heart.

> *Always giving thanks for all things in the name of our Lord Jesus Christ...* (Ephesians 5:20).

The Lord said to Job, *"Adorn yourself with glory and splendor, and clothe yourself in honor and majesty"* (Job 40:10 NIV). In the midst of Job's trials, God told Job to wrap himself in Glory and light and to cloak himself with honor and majesty. What we manifest in attitude and atmosphere will reproduce around us. Happiness is a choice. We choose to produce joy or depression. Which cloak will you wear today?

[CHAPTER 8]

THE TREE OF LIFE

In the beginning, Adam walked in the Garden of Eden with the Lord, who was the life of Adam. Perfectly united with the Lord, he walked and talked with Him daily, and had constant unbroken fellowship with Him. He enjoyed God with all of his being. The Lord freely gave Adam all things in the Garden, including free access to the Tree of Life, which he ate from daily.

Adam's sin severed his communion with the Lord. This had a catastrophic affect on Adam's spiritual and physical life; his very Life Source was severed, and he began to die. Had he not sinned, he would have enjoyed constant communion with God and would have lived forever.

> *And out of the ground the Lord God made to grow every*
> *tree that is pleasant to the sight or to be desired—good*
> *(suitable, pleasant) for food; the Tree of Life also in the*
> *center of the garden, and the tree of the knowledge of*
> *[the difference between] good and evil and blessing and*
> *calamity* (Genesis 2:9 AMP).

And the Lord God said, "Behold, the man has become like one of Us [The Father, Son, and Holy Spirit], to know [how to distinguish between] good and evil and blessing and calamity; and now, lest he put forth his hand and take also from the Tree of Life and eat, and live forever" (Genesis 3:22 AMP).

*So [God] drove out the man; and He placed at the east of the Garden of Eden the cherubim and a flaming sword which turned every way, to keep and guard **the way** to the Tree of Life* (Genesis 3:24 AMP).

Through the Cross, however, the veil was rent, and access to the presence of God was gained for all who believed. The Tree of Life was again available to humankind.

He who has an ear, let him hear what the Spirit says to the churches. To him who overcomes, I will grant to eat of the Tree of Life which is in the Paradise of God (Revelation 2:7).

Blessed are those who wash their robes, so that they may have the right to the Tree of Life, and may enter by the gates into the city (Revelation 22:14).

The *fruit* of the Tree of Life is God's unconditional love, and it's for our healing *now* because we will not need healing in Heaven.

To the Overcomers

We see in the Book of Revelation that instruction has been given to those who overcome.

He who is able to hear, let him listen to and give heed to what the Spirit says to the assemblies (churches). To him who overcomes (is victorious), I will grant to eat [of the fruit] of the Tree of Life, which is in the paradise of God (Revelation 2:7 AMP).

Through the middle of the broadway of the city; also, on either side of the river was the Tree of Life with its twelve varieties of fruit, yielding each month its fresh crop; and the leaves of the tree were for the healing and the restoration of the nations (Revelation 22:2 AMP).

Blessed (happy and to be envied) are those who cleanse their garments, that they may have the authority and right to [approach] the Tree of Life and to enter through the gates into the city (Revelation 22:14 AMP).

A river flows in the beginning of Creation and at the end of all things. We see the Tree of Life in the Garden in the beginning in Genesis and that same Tree of Life at the end of all things in Revelation 22.

There were two trees in the beginning of time. God said there are two ways we can take—the Tree of Life or the Tree of the Knowledge of Good and Evil. Two ways by which we live our lives as Christians—two ways we can go. There was the Tree of the Knowledge of Good and Evil—the knowledge of right and wrong. This tree essentially represented human ability to know right and wrong in the natural, completely independent of God. Thus, humanity, after the Fall, developed their soul life independent of God. They went their own way with their own powers.

Then there was the Tree of Life. The Tree of Life is Jesus. The Tree of Life represented relationship with the Lord and dependence on Him. One tree represented independence; the other tree represented relationship and dependence upon the Lord, who is the Way, the Truth, and the

Life. One required humans to live by their soul, and the other required them to live by their spirit.

When Adam chose the wrong tree, he chose to be independent of God. He chose to go his own way. Interestingly, satan came and said, "You can be as God." The implication is that you do not need to be dependent on God and that you can be as God. Adam's soul became his god.

Humanism now is the basic religion of the world—people are as God. Humanity can find its own way. When Adam chose his own way he lost Eden; he lost the presence of God; he lost relationship with Him—he lost paradise. From then on, he would be working out of his own independent soul life, and he would have to find his own way. He would have to make his own paradise by natural strengths and abilities. Humanity has been striving to that end ever since.

Spiritual Life

The Tree of Life offered spiritual life for Adam and was the life-giving flow of supernatural connection between Heaven and earth. When Adam took of the wrong tree, he exercised his free will, and in this fallen state of his knowledge of evil, innocence was lost. If he had taken of the Tree of Life in this fallen state, he would have lived forever as a fallen man. This is why the Lord God had to put Adam and Eve out of the Garden of Eden, even placing two angels there to guard access to "the Way" to the Tree of Life.

Where is the Tree of Life Now? It is in Heaven.

> *He who is able to hear, let him listen to and give heed to what the Spirit says to the assemblies (churches). To him who overcomes (is victorious), I will grant to eat [of the fruit] of the Tree of Life, which is in the paradise of God* (Revelation 2:7 AMP).

After the flood, paradise on earth was lost. It disappeared. Now, in the endtime, we see a picture of this tree in paradise in Heaven. This Tree of Life is the Lord Jesus Christ. He *is* the Tree of Life. However, it is evident that not all Christians have access to this tree—to this aspect of God's life, this experience of Jesus. It says those *who overcome* will have access to this Tree of Life. When the overcomers eat of the tree, they will live forever. The last enemy to be destroyed is death (see 1 Cor. 15:26).

One of the purposes of the Tree of Life was for the healing of the nations (see Rev. 22:2). The time is now for this tree to blossom in our lives and in the Church of Jesus Christ again so that the nations may be healed. Jesus alluded to the tree while speaking to His disciples:

> *I am the vine, you are the branches; he who abides in Me*
> *and I in him, he bears much fruit* (John 15:5).

He said that we were to dwell in Him and that He would dwell in us. When we live in Him, He will live in us: *"As the branch cannot bear fruit of itself unless it abides in the vine, so neither can you unless you abide in Me"* (John 15:4).

We have the awesome privilege of becoming a branch of this tree who is the Lord Jesus Christ, and this "Tree" is for the healing of the nations. The only way we can bear fruit for the healing of the nations is to abide in Him. How do we abide?

> *If you keep My commandments, you will abide in My*
> *love; just as I have kept My Father's commandments and*
> *abide in His love* (John 15:10).

It is clear that if we keep His commandments, we abide in Him. He chose and appointed us—planted us that we might bear fruit (and lasting fruit at that) so that whatever we ask the Father in Jesus' name, we might receive it (see John 15:16). This lasting fruit is for the healing of the nations. There has been much pruning. If we continue to abide in Jesus, that is, to live and to stay in love with Him, keeping His commandments, we will bring forth fruit. I believe that this Tree of Life flowing in us is about to yield great and glorious fruit.

The River of Life

The River of Life flows from the throne of God into the earth. Everything that it touches is healed. The Bible tells us in Revelation that this river waters the Tree of Life, that it is a pure river like crystal, flowing from the throne of God and of the Lamb (see Rev. 22:1).

This supernatural river is the one that came out of Eden, the one that watered and fed the Tree, healing everything it touched. God planted it in the east—in Eden. The Bible specifies not that the Lord planted the Garden of Eden, but that the Lord planted a *garden in the East,* in Eden. Eden was the *entrance point* or pathway for the spirit world to come through, the supernatural door which bridged the spirit and the natural and physical realms (see Gen. 2:8).

According to Genesis 2:10, the river went *"out of Eden"* to water the Garden and from there, it divided. Revelation 22:1 says that the river flows out from the throne of God and on either side of the river is the Tree of Life. It bears twelve varieties of fruit yielding a fresh crop every month.

This same river flowed out from the throne in Genesis through Eden's door to water the Tree of Life in the middle of the Garden. Adam saw all of these things and was amazed. Not only did he see the river flow through this supernatural passageway that connected Heaven and earth, but he saw the angelic hosts and heavenly creatures pass through as well. Adam was just as enveloped with the hosts of Heaven as he was with his natural surroundings. That life-giving crystal river flowed from that heavenly portal called Eden.

Life-Giving River of Love

It is important to understand that God is both Love and Light. It is not that He gives life and gives love. He *is* love and He *is* life.

And we know (understand, recognize, are conscious of, by observation and by experience) and believe (adhere to and put faith in and rely on) the love God cherishes for us. God is love, and he who dwells and continues in love dwells and continues in God, and God dwells and continues in him (1 John 4:16 AMP).

This is the message we have heard from Him and announce to you, that God is Light, and in Him there is no darkness at all (1 John 1:5).

Love and light are powers. They are energies. This life-giving river is a pure river of love, and that love becomes incredible light that has the power to heal, to restore, and to transform. It becomes a river of the love of God, and when we drink of it, we become beings of light—sons and daughters of light, dispersing and flowing in light. Until we are flowing in this river—unless it flows out from us—we will not have access to the Tree of Life for the healing of nations.

. . . Jesus stood, and He cried in a loud voice, "If any man is thirsty, let him come to Me and drink! He who believes in Me [who cleaves to and trusts in and relies on Me] as the Scripture has said, from his innermost being shall flow [continuously] **springs** *and* **rivers** *of living water"* (John 7:37- 38 AMP).

In the beginning, Genesis had a river; at the end, Revelation has a river; and in the middle of human history, Jesus Christ came to open up that which was shut off—a new and living "Way," the River of Life. Out of us shall flow "rivers" and "springs" of living water. Out of our innermost being will flow rivers of life. What is that life? What is that river? It is the river of love. The Body of Christ in the earth will flow in love. This flow of faith that works by love will heal the nations (see Gal. 5:6).

Because of this flow of love, the Tree of Life will bloom in these endtimes, for there has been a lot of pruning of the human condition. God is preparing a people who manifest this Tree of Life from their innermost being.

We need to ask ourselves some questions! What is flowing out of me? What *kind* of light is flowing out of me? Is it a bright brilliant light or a dim, dark light? In the spirit realm, demons and angels see it and know exactly what we are by the brilliance or dimness of that light. Wherever we go, we leave behind a trail of light. We affect people by what we emanate. If we emanate love's light, it will be so bright that it will transform your life and the people you touch. Why? Because love is an essence, a power, and life. For example, when a person dies, he or she leaves behind a trail of what has emanated from his or her life both negative and positive. Yes, we will leave behind a deposit in this world of the things, people, and circumstances we have touched. Nobody lives or dies unto himself (see Rom. 14:7). We have an affect on this life, on creation, on our world in which we live.

Unless we learn to live, dwell, and abide in love, we cannot abide in Him. In these endtimes, this tree will bear fruit in the Church that will flow out of a river of love for the healing of the nations of the world. The creative DNA of the Father will be released through a genetically transformed Body of Christ that moves and flows in the currents of love. Creative miracles and supernatural ability will be the distinguishing mark of those who have been transformed by this power of light and love. Even creation will see it and respond to it. The earth, the wind, the elements, and all life will see it and become responsive and obedient to this unique people group.

> *And I heard, but I did not understand. Then I said, "O my Lord, what shall be the issue and final end of these things?" And he [the angel] said, "Go your way, Daniel, for the words are shut up and sealed till the time of the end"* (Daniel 12:8-9 AMP).

The secrets were sealed until the time of the end, but in Daniel 12:3 the angel said that the knowledge would increase, that the wise would understand and shine, and that they would turn many to righteousness.

Angels Guard the "Way"

Two cherubim guarded the entrance to the Garden of Eden—the "Way" to "the Tree of Life" after the expulsion of Adam and Eve (see Gen. 3:24). Cherubim are winged angelic creatures. Ezekiel actually had a curious encounter with cherubim and gave us a good description of their appearance. They were winged creatures covered and completely full of eyes, as were their four "whirling" wheels. Each of the cherubim had four faces: One face was that of a cherub, the second the face of a man, the third the face of a lion, and the fourth the face of an eagle. (See Ezekiel 1; 10:12-14.)

Do you know that God instructed Moses to make two cherubim out of hammered gold on the top of the two ends of the mercy seat on the Ark of the Covenant? They were to have their wings spread upward, overshadowing the cover with them, facing each other, and looking toward the cover, according to Exodus 25:18-20.

> *Moses said to Aaron, "Take a jar and put an omerful of manna in it, and place it before the Lord to be kept throughout your generations"* (Exodus 16:33).

So they took manna and placed it in the Ark of the Covenant. What did those two cherubim guard? They guarded the way to the mercy seat, to the hidden manna, to the "Tree of Life." Guess what? The Israelites lived for 40 years without growing old or dying. Their clothing did not wear out and there was not one feeble among them. They lived for 40 years on this supernatural food called manna without changing—without growing old.

The Way to the Mercy Seat

This is the Bread which came down out of Heaven; not as the fathers ate and died; he who eats this Bread will live forever (John 6:58).

The cover was the mercy seat and signified "atonement" or "covering." Jesus died on the Cross and the veil was rent, giving us *access* to the mercy seat. The "Way" to the mercy seat was opened up to humanity again because God so loved the world. Love opened the Way. The love of God opened the lid to the manna of the Tree of Life—that hidden manna, Christ Jesus.

> *He who is able to hear, let him listen to and heed what the Spirit says to the assemblies (churches). To him who overcomes (conquers), I will give to eat of the manna that is hidden, and I will give him a white stone with a new name engraved on the stone, which no one knows or understands except he who receives it* (Revelation 2:17 AMP).

Access to the Tree of Life is given to those who overcome, said the angel to the Church at Ephesus. The church had lost her first love. The angel was saying that if they repented and returned to their first love, they would be allowed to eat of the fruit of the Tree of Life in the Paradise of God.

Key to the Garden

In Rick Joyner's book *The Final Quest,* Joyner describes a panoramic vision given to him on February 16, 1995, that continued over a period of one year. In the first part of this vision, Joyner saw a great army from hell that had been released against the Church. He saw the degree to which this evil has its grip on believers, how many Christians are being used by the enemy, and what it will take to set them free. Here is an excerpt from the second part of the vision, described as the "high way" where a unified, glorious Church rises up as a great army in the most pivotal battle of all time between light and darkness. As they fought, they ascended to different levels of a mountain.

> For a long time we continued killing vultures and picking off the demons that were riding on the Christians. We found that arrows of different truths would have different impact on different demons. We knew that it was going to be a long battle, but we were not suffering casualties anymore now, and we had continued to climb past the level of patience. Even so, after these Christians had the demons shot off them few would come to the mountain, because many had taken on the nature of the demons and had continued in their delusion without them. As the darkness of these demons dissipated, we could see the ground moving around the feet of these Christians. Then I saw that their legs had been bound by serpents. I kept looking at the serpents and could see they were all the same kind and had the same name on them, which was "shame." We shot arrows of truth at the serpents, but they had little effect. We then tried the arrows of hope, but without any results. From Galatians 2:20 it would have been so easy to go higher, because we all helped each other. Since there seemed to be little we could do against these serpents and against the enemy, we decided to keep climbing as far as we could until we found something that would work against these serpents. We passed levels of truth very fast. On most of them we did not even bother to look around if there was not a weapon apparent that

would work on these serpents. Faith, hope, and love had stayed right with us, but I had not noticed that we had left wisdom far behind. It would be a long time before I would understand what a mistake this was. He would catch up with us on the top of the mountain. But, leaving him behind cost us a much quicker and easier victory over the evil horde.[1]

Then they happened upon a very interesting entranceway that they felt compelled to enter.

Almost without warning we came into a level that opened up into a garden. It was the most beautiful place I had ever seen in my life. Over the entrance to this garden was written, "The Father's unconditional love." This entrance was so glorious and so inviting we just could not resist entering. As soon as I entered, I saw a tree that I knew was the Tree of Life. It was in the middle of this garden and it was still guarded by angels of awesome power and authority. When I looked at them, they looked back. They seemed friendly, as if they had been expecting us. I looked back and now there was a host of other warriors behind me in the garden. This gave us all courage, and because of the angels' attitudes toward us, we decided to pass them and get to the tree. One of the angels called out, "Those who make it to this level and those who know the Father's love can eat of this tree." I did not realize how hungry I was. When I tasted the fruit it was better than anything I had tasted before. But it was also somehow familiar. It brought memories. Memories straightaway began to flood my soul, memories of sunshine and rain and beautiful fields and sun setting over the ocean. But even more than that of people that I loved. With every bite I loved everything and everyone more. Then, my enemies started coming to mind. I loved them, too. The feeling was soon greater than anything I had ever experienced, even the peace of Galatians 2:20 when we had reached that level. Then I heard the voice of the Lord saying, "This is now your daily bread. It shall never be withheld from you. You may eat as much and often as you like. There is no end to My love." I looked up at the tree to see who had spoken this. I saw that the tree was filled with pure, white eagles. They had the most beautiful, penetrating eyes I had ever seen. They were looking at me as if waiting for instructions. One of the angels said, "They will do your bidding and these eagles eat snakes." I said, "Go, deliver your Christians. Deliver your people. Go devour the shame that has bound our brothers." And they opened their wings and a great wind came, and they lifted up from the air. These eagles filled the sky with a blinding glory; even as high as we were I could hear the sounds and terror from the enemies' camps at the sight of the eagles ascending.[2]

The doorway into this garden was the Father's unconditional love. The level they had reached was the knowledge of the Father's love, and it was at this level that they could partake of the Tree of Life. Only when they had reached this place in God could they then release their brethren who were still bound in the earth.

Now, listen to me carefully. God is bringing forth a people in these last days who will know the Father's love, who will know what it means to walk in love, give love, be love, and receive love. They will be a people who will literally become love, whereby love flows from them as light and begins to restore and heal the nations. It is coming in our day.

As we approach the end of this age, we will see tremendous things. Knowledge and understanding will be released as never before into an era of millennium technology that will transform the world. We will take this technology to the nations, and it will transform them and give them a better standard of living, yes, but most of all, we will bring with it the Father's love. And the nations will heal. I believe we will see entire nations healed in a tremendous, awesome move of God. I believe God is going to do such a great work in our day that if He showed us even a glimpse we wouldn't be able to believe or comprehend it.

The Word of the Lord is: "I have been pruning this tree for a long time—this Tree of Life. My people will become a branch in the earth of the Tree of Life to bring healing and love to the nations."

Listen—it is not enough to preach the Gospel. We have to bring love. It is not enough to say, "Jesus loves you," when they are hungry. "Come into the Kingdom of God, and God will help all of you," is not adequate any longer. Been there, done that. It does not work in places like India anymore. We have to *actively* love these people by lifting their standards and making life more bearable for them.

The Light of Love

God will have a people who are trees of righteousness in the last days. If you desire to be one of those, then you must abide in, walk in, and bear the fruit of love for transformation. God is love and love will transform you. When love flows from you, it is transformed into a power of light. When love turns into light and the light passes through you, you will experience that healing and transformation. Power—the light of God—will charge through every atom of your being because love becomes a fantastic power of light. In that light are healing, revelation, knowledge, understanding, and insight. Flowing from your mind and your lips will be love.

When your mind and lips lose the power to hurt, you will gain access to the Tree of Life. Only those who overcome the darkness will eat of the Tree. *"A gentle tongue [with its healing power] is a tree of life, but willful contrariness in it breaks down the spirit"* (Proverbs 15:4 AMP). The King James Version of this verse is "A wholesome tongue is a tree of life: but perverseness therein is a breach in the spirit."

One definition for the word *breach* is "a break in relations." In the above verse it means to be *cut off from abiding in Him.* A wholesome tongue transmits a tree of life, but perverseness will cause a breach in the spirit; this breach cuts you off from God and His love flowing through you.

The mouth is the clearest revelation of someone's heart.

> *The good man out of the good treasure of his heart brings forth what is good; and the evil man out of the evil treasure brings forth what is evil; for his mouth speaks from that which fills his heart* (Luke 6:45).

Seek Perfection in Love

To grow and flow in love, do not seek power—seek God, hear God, fill your heart with God. Then love will flow out of you—out of your mouth, out of your words, out of your entire being. We give ourselves away when we open our mouths; if the light and love of God is inside, the light and love will flow out of you. Seek transformation by being thankful in all things as you learn to walk in love. Love must be your desire, your goal. When you seek love, God will give you the power to love with all of your heart. When you seek to be perfected in love, God will perfect you in love and give you great power—power with which to love. All too often we get it the other way around, but the apostle Paul said in First Corinthians 12:31 that although we are to earnestly desire and zealously cultivate the greatest and best gifts and graces, there was a more excellent way—the way of love.

How vital is this way of love in our lives? Those who know the Father's love have access to the Tree of Life. This company of believers who flow in love will access that garden and take of the fruit of the Tree of Life. They will have the power to destroy the serpents that blind humanity from seeing and knowing God. The god of this world has blinded the unbelievers' minds so that they cannot discern the truth, so that they cannot see the light of the Gospel of the Glory of the Messiah who is the image and likeness of God (see 2 Cor. 4:4). We are bearers of His Image.

God is removing the Church's blinders so that we might truly understand the depth of who we are as Image-bearers. As His seed, we must recall that the seed bears the original genetics of reproduction; it bears the original design. As the saying goes, "You can count the seeds in an apple, but you cannot count the apples in a seed."

The Lord is preparing a people who understand this—those who understand their original design and who will gain right of access to the Tree of Life in the Garden. Those ones will not be looking to make great names for themselves but to become beacons of light and love who reveal Christ to their generation. God will entrust great power for the healing and restoration of the nations to that Glory generation of people who move in love, compassion, and humility.

There is a God in Heaven who reveals secrets—what shall be in the latter days. I believe we are entering into the end of the age, into the latter days when the secrets of God are being revealed. This is what Rick Joyner discovered in his vision, as he relayed in his account, when he finally arrived at the top of the mountain. He saw the gate at the doorway and the angel told him, "You can only eat of the Tree if you know the Father's unconditional love."

Jesus has opened wide that door, and the invitation to eat once more from the Tree of Life is for those who, by choice, have cut that Adamic taproot to the soul life to derive their life source from the Tree of Life. Jesus said He is the "Way," the "Truth," and the "Life." He is the Way to life eternal. We must eat of His body and drink of His blood, for He is the great Tree of Life—our Life Source.

The river of love is the gateway to the Garden and to the fruit of the Tree of Life, whose branches will heal the nations. The love of God flowing through His people will reveal the hidden manna—Christ Jesus—to the World.

Power of Communion

In this hour, the government of God is being established in the earth. There is a solidifying process taking place in the Body of Christ. We are being cemented into Christ—His nature in our nature. From this place of *oneness*, there is a remnant of believers rising to a new level—a people of great faith, a rising Glory generation emerging from the desert, a people who know their God and do great exploits (see Dan. 11:32). In order for us to move into the next season, we must first come to know and practice *the lasting value and power of communion.*

Exchanging Realms

People often receive communion in a ritualistic manner—taking the body and blood of Jesus out of routine and tradition. In order for us to taste the richness of communion, there must be a time of preparation where we are lifted into the Glory of His presence through the worship of who He is. Just like it's not possible for us to effectively *wait* in the presence of the Lord until we have passed from the natural realm into the spiritual, so we cannot effectively receive the value and substance of the body and blood of Jesus until we first exchange realms—earth for Heaven.

The word *communion* has to do with *communication*—Jesus speaks and we listen; we speak, He listens. As we enter into communion with Jesus we become *one* with Him. We actually become partakers of life because He is Life.

> *Therefore there is now no condemnation for those who are in Christ Jesus. For the law of the Spirit of life in Christ*

Jesus has set you free from the law of sin and of death
(Romans 8:1-2).

This *condemnation* is the judgment (death) which was given Adam for his transgression and was, in turn, passed on to each of us. However, we are set free from the *law of sin* through our identification with the *shed blood* of Jesus on the Cross. We are set free from the *law of sin and death* by the *Spirit of Life* through our identification with the *resurrection* and *ascension* of Jesus.

A Life-Giving Spirit

The Scriptures tell us, "The first man, Adam, became a living person." But the last Adam—that is, Christ—is a life-giving Spirit (1 Corinthians 15:45 NLT).

Jesus said that He came that we might have life and have it *more abundantly* (see John 10:10). We become partakers of the *law of the Spirit* through our identification with Him as a life-giving Spirit. When this happens we don't just receive life in our spirits and minds, but in our physical bodies as well.

In John 6, Jesus multiplied five barley loaves and two fish, feeding over 5,000 men, yet when they became hungry again, they came back to Jesus looking for more food. But Jesus told them He had something better for them, saying:

...unless you eat the flesh of the Son of Man and drink His blood, you have no life in yourselves....This is the bread which came down out of Heaven; not as the fathers ate and died; he who eats this bread will live forever (John 6:53,58).

Jesus was offering them a higher life in which they would not die. He was showing them that another serving of barley loaves and fish wouldn't suffice, but rather only His flesh and blood—bread from Heaven that gives eternal life.

Eternal Life in the Now

When Jesus said we would live forever, we know He was talking about eternal life in God's Kingdom. However, we can receive this eternal life *now* as we abide in His presence here on the earth.

> *Abide in Me, and I in you. As the branch cannot bear fruit of itself unless it abides in the vine, so neither can you unless you abide in Me. I am the vine...* (John 15:4-5).

When a strip of bark is completely cut around a tree and removed, the process of death begins. The tree can no longer receive the life and nourishment that is drawn up from the root system and passes through the bark; the tree will soon die. Similarly, the life of Jesus must flow into us. We are the branches and He is the Vine. We only receive the *power of endless life* if we are rightly connected to Him.

> *...who has come, not according to the law of a fleshly commandment, but according to the power of an endless life* (Hebrews 7:16 NKJV).

Eating food to sustain our natural body is not an option; it's something we need to do to stay alive. Likewise, partaking of the Lord is not an option; it's necessary to stay wholly alive in spirit, soul, and body. Receiving the body and blood of Jesus is more than taking communion once a month at church—we must partake daily from the table He has set before us. If we don't, we will suffer loss spiritually and naturally.

I used to think Adam had eternal existence built within him when he was created; however, Adam was created when the life and breath of

God was breathed into him. In order for him to stay alive, he had to continually come to the Tree of Life and eat from it. He was dependent on God and needed to dine on His life. After Adam sinned, he was not allowed to eat from the Tree of Life.

> *Then the Lord God said, "Behold, the man has become like one of Us, knowing good and evil; and now, he might stretch out his hand, and take also from the tree of life, and eat, and live forever...." So He drove the man out; and at the east of the garden of Eden He stationed the cherubim and the flaming sword which turned every direction to guard the way to the tree of life* (Genesis 3:22,24).

After Adam transgressed he was cut off from communion, from eating from the Tree of Life. If he had continued eating, he would have continued living. But the judgment was not being allowed to eat from the Tree of Life, resulting in spiritual and physical death.

The Right to Eat

> *...To him who overcomes, I will grant to eat of the tree of life which is in the Paradise of God* (Revelation 2:7).

Those who overcome have access to eat from the Tree of Life in the Paradise of God. Once again we see that we have access to the Tree of Life, to the Bread of Life, to abundant life, to eternal life through the broken body and shed blood of Jesus Christ. When we partake of communion, the way to the Tree of Life is opened to us—we have access to His resurrection power and life.

Earlier we talked about how Jesus multiplied the loaves of bread and fish to feed the multitude of people; then the following day, the people sought Jesus looking for more food (see John 6:1-26). Jesus explained to them that they would never be truly filled unless they ate His flesh and drank His blood (see John 6:53). The people didn't understand and some were offended. Then the night before His crucifixion, He took His disciples aside and openly explained in more detail about the power released through His shed blood and broken body.

> *He...took bread; and when He had given thanks, He broke it and said, "This is My body, which is for you; do this in remembrance of Me." In the same way He took the cup also after supper, saying, "This cup is the new covenant in My blood; do this, as often as you drink it, in remembrance of Me"* (1 Corinthians 11:23-25).

Notice that Jesus said that the bread was His body and the cup was His blood. He didn't say that it was an *emblem* or a *symbol*, but it was His very body and blood.

> *... Truly I say to you, unless you are converted and become like children, you will not enter the Kingdom of Heaven* (Matthew 18:3).

As we take communion, we see bread, but Jesus said it was His body. As we take the cup, we see the fruit of the vine, but Jesus said it was His blood. Having the mind of a child, we simply believe what Jesus said—not what we see.

The "Mystical" Tree of Life

Jesus is the mystic secret of God; all spiritual knowledge and enlightenment are hidden in Christ.

> *...that they... may know more definitely and accurately and thoroughly that mystic secret of God, [which is] Christ (the Anointed One). In Him all the treasures of [divine] wisdom (comprehensive insight into the ways and purposes of God) and [all the riches of spiritual] knowledge and*

enlightenment are stored up and lie hidden (Colossians 2:2-3 AMP).

In His ascension, Jesus opened the way for us to partake of His life-giving Spirit. We have access to Jesus, the mystical Tree of Life, who resides in paradise.

> *For He* [Jesus] *shall grow up before Him as a tender plant, and as a root* [Tree of Life] *out of dry ground. He has no form or comeliness; and when we see Him, there is no beauty that we should desire Him* (Isaiah 53:2 NKJV).

Taking communion by faith gives us understanding; it opens our eyes to see Jesus as the Tree of Life. If we partake without believing and knowing that He is Life, we rob ourselves of the life that Christ offers us and all we do is eat the bread and drink the fruit of the vine and it's just another good meal. If we partake with spiritual understanding (worthily), knowing that we are taking in the life of Christ, then by faith we will no longer be weak or sick, nor will we die prematurely. Rather, we will live longer, healthier lives, revived and rejuvenated by the life-giving Spirit of Christ.

> *...He who raised Christ Jesus from the dead will also give life to your mortal bodies through His Spirit who dwells in you* (Romans 8:11).

We need to ask the Holy Spirit to awaken these truths in our hearts, quickening them, allowing us to identify with the death and resurrection of Christ. When I take communion, I normally speak something to the Lord like this:

> *"Lord, as I receive the bread, I identify with Your body that was broken. Your body bore stripes, and through the*

blood that flowed from those stripes, I receive healing. Your body was broken on the Cross. I identify with Your broken body and receive forgiveness of sin. Lord, as I take the cup, the fruit of the vine, I identify with resurrection and ascension power released through Your blood. It is the cup of a New Covenant—the power of an endless life. I identify with You being the Tree of Life—I release my body from the power of death and receive longevity of life."

Living in the Glory of God

When God led the children of Israel out of Egyptian slavery and through the desert, there was not a single feeble person among them. They were supernaturally sustained in the Glory of God. As long as they ate the bread that came from Heaven, their bodies, clothing, shoes, and all they possessed did not corrupt or age. The molecular structure of all they owned and possessed was kept new and fresh. As they ate the bread of angels, they were kept from sickness (see Ps. 78:25). Joshua said that he was as strong at the end of the 40 years of walking through the desert as he was when he left Egypt—he was over 80 years old! Talk about living in the Glory of God.

Just as Adam needed to come to the Tree of Life to eat and live, we must do the same. When we partake of the Tree of Life, we will live the fullness of time that has been given to us. People are looking beyond liturgical religious forms—pressing past routine worship into a spiritual reality. There is a fresh hunger for the living God. By faith believers are pressing through by partaking of the flesh and blood of Jesus—eating from the Tree of Life.

"Lord, help us understand these profound yet simple mysteries of communion. Thank You for opening up a new and living way for us—giving us direct access into Your

presence so we can freely partake of the Tree of Life. By faith we desire to partake of Your flesh and blood, receiving all the life, power, and healing within. We identify with Your death, with Your broken body and shed blood, dying ourselves to this world and to its laws, and being wholly and unconditionally released from the power and influence of death. All for the Glory of the Lord Jesus Christ. Amen."

Endnotes

1.   Rick Joyner, *The Final Quest* (New Kensington, PA: Whitaker House, 1997), 33-34.

2.   Ibid., 34.

[CHAPTER 9]

SUPERNATURAL PATHWAYS

There is a strong emphasis coming into the Body of Christ in this next season of time that will quickly become the hallmark theme of everything that we as believers are to become. This Kingdom reality will be the cornerstone of truth that will anchor the Church of Jesus Christ to its original mandate, propelling the Church into a reawakening of sonship marked by powerful displays of the miraculous. This will in turn lead to the beginning of transformation of churches, cities, regions, and whole nations. This reawakening is *Christ in us,* the hope of Glory.

Paul wrote to the church at Ephesus and said

> His [Jesus'] intention was the perfecting and the full equipping of the saints (His consecrated people), [that they should do] the work of ministering toward building up Christ's Body (the Church)...until we all attain oneness in the faith and in the comprehension of the [full and

accurate] knowledge of the Son of God, that [we might arrive] at really mature manhood [the NKJV says "a perfect man"]...*the measure of the stature of the fullness of the Christ and the completeness found in Him* (Ephesians 4:12-13 AMP).

Paul also prayed for the Galatian church. He wrote, *"My little children, for whom I am again suffering birth pangs until Christ is completely and permanently formed (molded) within you* (Gal. 4:19 AMP).

There is maturing taking place—a coming to fullness of all things both good and evil. Things that we have known in a limited measure in the past are going to come to fullness and be made known. For example, we now have a limited measure and understanding of the gifts of the Spirit, the prophetic anointing, and different levels of authority. However, God is bringing us to the fullness of its measure as mature sons and daughters who rightly represent Him in the earth. This maturing will happen as God's seed is sown into the good ground of our hearts, and a powerful manifestation of Christ in us will come forth like never before.

God's Creative Nature in Man

In the beginning God (prepared, formed, fashioned, and) created the heavens and the earth. The earth was without form and an empty waste, and darkness was upon the face of the very great deep. The Spirit of God was moving (hovering, brooding) over the face of the waters. And God said, "Let there be light"; and there was light (Genesis 1:1-3 AMP).

The Hebrew word used to describe God here is *Elohim*, which means "Creator." Adam was born from Creator God with His likeness and ability in the earth. Even though in the natural it was impossible for

Adam to tend and keep the Garden, I propose to you that supernaturally Adam was completely equipped to do the job. Like his Father, *Elohim,* Adam simply "spoke," and it was created and done.

Little "god" Man

If the prevailing law of creation is that everything brings forth after its own kind, then tell me, what was Adam really like? What kind of son did God actually bring forth? More importantly, what was it that was really lost in the Garden of Eden, and what was it that Jesus Christ came to restore to us? To answer this more fully, let's look at an encounter that Jesus had with the Jewish leaders of His day. They asked Him to tell them plainly if He was indeed the Christ, and Jesus answered them like this.

> *"I and the Father are One." Again the Jews brought up stones to stone Him. Jesus said to them, "My Father has enabled Me to do many good deeds. [I have shown many acts of mercy in your presence]* [supernatural acts of miracles]. *For which of these do you mean to stone Me?" The Jews replied, "We are not going to stone You for a good act* [for doing supernatural acts], *but for blasphemy, because You, a mere Man, make Yourself [out to be] God. Jesus answered, "Is it not written in your Law, 'I said, You are gods'? So men are called gods [by the law], men to whom God's message came—and the Scripture cannot be set aside or cancelled or broken or annulled"* (John 10:30-35 AMP).

Did you hear what Jesus said? He said, "Men are called gods. To these men God's message came, and the Scripture cannot be set aside, or cancelled, or broken, or annulled."

The good deeds Jesus was doing were supernatural works of power in miracles and the healing of the sick. In essence Jesus was saying to them, "Why do you accuse Me of acting like God when we are all His earthly representatives and are to act on God's behalf? Should we not all be doing great works of power since God has given the earth to man to rule as little 'gods'?"

> *The heavens are the Lord's heavens, but the earth has He given to the children of men* (Psalm 115:16 AMP).

> *God stands in the assembly [of the representatives] of God; in the midst of the magistrates or judges He gives judgment [as] among the gods...I said, You are gods [since you judge on My behalf, as My representatives]; indeed, all of you are children of the Most High* (Psalms 82:1,6 AMP)

Jesus was quoting Psalm 82:6, saying that we are gods (small "g"). This means rulers, judges, divine ones, God-like ones, or mighty ones. Interestingly, *Elohim* is the same word for "God" and "god." We are God's "creator gods" on the earth, establishing His earthly government as ambassadors of His supernatural Kingdom. Everything brings forth after its own kind—we are His offspring, made in His image. We are of the same family and species as God.

The word *image* means *"a reproduction or imitation of the form of a person or thing, a tangible or visible representation,* or an *exact likeness."*[1] Jesus was the image of the invisible of God. He declared boldly, *"He who has seen Me has seen the Father"* (John 14:9).

Jesus and the Father are One. He is the outshining of His Glory, the projection of the invisible God—and we are "imago deo," made in His image and likeness. As we abide in Him and He in us, we have access into the heavens and are able to move in power and authority on the earth.

> *But to as many as did receive and welcome Him, He gave the authority (power, privilege, right) to become the*

children of God, that is, to those who believe in (adhere to, trust in, and rely on) His name (John 1:12 AMP).

Jesus didn't shed His blood on the Cross just so we could go to Heaven when we die. Jesus Christ came to restore total access to the Father, which was lost through the Fall. Now through the blood of Jesus, God has opened to us a new and living way. He has restored to us the long-lost relationship title deed of "Sons of God."

When Christ stepped into us, we took on a new *nature;* we were, in essence, recreated in an instant. We must understand that man was not created simply to serve, but to rule and reign on earth. We were, in fact, created by Father God to be the "gods of this world." God longs for us to begin to understand His nature and His ways. He wants us to take dominion over the elements, sin, sickness, disease, and death, exercising our God-given authority.

When I believe that I possess His Spirit, I am able to administrate His dominion—I have something tangible that I can give. Outside of the gate called Beautiful, Peter approached the lame beggar and said:

Silver and gold I do not have, but what I do have I give you: In the name of Jesus Christ of Nazareth, rise up and walk (Acts 3:6 NKJV).

Peter took the crippled man by the hand, and immediately his feet and ankle bones received strength. Peter knew he had something to give. I also have something to give—the same Spirit that raised Christ from the dead dwells in me. We are joint heirs to the throne with Jesus—we have something to give away.

Satan's Lie

From the beginning, satan has desperately tried to keep this Kingdom truth hidden from humankind. Satan could never compete with a son of God, and he knew he could never become a son. Angels could never compete with this position. Satan is only an angel; he is not of the same family as we are. Lucifer was insanely jealous of man, and he came up with a lie to hide the fact that man was the *family* of *God* made in His *likeness*. Today we simply call that lie "evolution." Lucifer knew if he could get us to just believe that we evolved from a lower species then he could continue to separate us from God's family. Lucifer was never a son, and he set out to destroy the human race—the sons and daughters of God.

Since the Fall, humankind has lived from the realm of the soul, cut off from the realm of the spirit. But Jesus Christ restored access to the spirit realm by destroying sin in the flesh.

A New and Living Way

Jesus Christ came into the world to restore humanity to their original position of sonship by a new and living way.

> *Therefore, brethren, since we have full freedom and confidence to enter into the [Holy of] Holies [by the power and virtue] in the blood of Jesus, by this fresh (new) and living way which He initiated and dedicated and opened for us through the separating curtain (veil of the Holy of Holies), that is, through His flesh* (Hebrews 10:19-20 AMP).

Jesus opened the heavenlies through the veil of His flesh. The first Adam lost his way in the Garden of Eden along with all of his privileges and rights, but Jesus Christ, the second Adam, restored all things to us including full governmental authority with all of its rights, privileges, and power. Finally the long lost title deed of "children of God" was returned to humankind.

Branded Sons of God

When Adam and Eve were brought forth, God had a family—a son and a daughter. Think about what this really meant to God. He had a family in the earth.

We know that through the Fall humanity gave up their position and in turn became the children of the enemy and took on his likeness and his image. But through the Cross and the blood of Jesus, God has remedied the situation.

> But to as many as did received and welcome Him, He gave the authority (power, privilege, right) to become the children of God, that is, to those who believe in (adhere to, trust in, and rely on) His name. Who owe their birth neither to bloods nor to the will of the flesh [that of physical impulse] nor to the will of man [that of a natural father], but to God. [They are born of God!] (John 1:12-13 AMP).

When Paul wrote to the church at Ephesus and Galatia telling them that his intention for them was the perfecting and full equipping of the saints until they arrived at really mature manhood, he was bearing all of the history and design of humanity in mind. Paul was telling them in Galatians 4:19 that he was actually suffering birth pangs in himself until Christ was completely and permanently formed, or molded, within them.

There is a maturing taking place—a coming to fullness of all things, both good and evil. We are at the end of the age, and the seeds of the Kingdom sown in our hearts are coming to age and maturity. The things we have known in a limited measure will be made fully known. This reawakening Body of Christ is coming forth in the full power of Heaven and will fill the whole earth with the knowledge of the Glory of God. This is the Church's finest hour. This is the final curtain in the show of the human race, and children of the Kingdom will shine like none other in history. God always saves the best for last, and this shining forth will be none other that *Christ in us,* the hope of Glory!

> *To whom God was pleased to make known how great for the Gentiles are the riches of the glory of this mystery, which is* **Christ within and among you, the Hope of [realizing the] glory** (Colossians 1:27 AMP).

The Mystic Realm

Christ is the great Mystic Secret of God in whom all the treasures of divine wisdom are stored up and lie hidden:

> *...that they may become progressively more intimately acquainted with and may know more definitely and accurately and thoroughly that* **mystic secret of God, [which is] Christ** *(the Anointed One). In Him all the treasures of* **[divine] wisdom** *(comprehensive insight into the ways and purposes of God) and [all the riches of* **spiritual] knowledge and enlightenment** *are stored up and lie hidden* (Colossians 2:2-3 AMP).

> *Thus says the Lord: Stand by the roads and look; and ask for the eternal paths, where the good, old way is; then walk in it, and you will find rest for your souls* (Jeremiah 6:16 AMP).

Ancient Pathways

The Bible is clear that there are roads that lead to eternal paths, and we are to ask the Lord for them to lead us in the good, old way. These ancient pathways were established at the creation of the world and are meant for us to walk so we can find rest for our souls. Adam was lead by these pathways to the Garden of Eden, and he moved on these supernatural highways. Though some would argue, these heavenly roads are still open and available for us today, but there are few who find them. Jesus opened up this new and living way for us so we can come boldly into the throne room of grace. He spilled His blood not only to save humankind, but to give us access into His very presence. This access into the throne room is Heaven's highway system.

In the following pages you will hear testimonies of those that have been transported into various locations by the Spirit of God. Transportations and translocations are divine acts of God that physically or spiritually move an individual into different places in this time or another. Peter was in a secure prison and was delivered by from jail by an angel that opened a portal in the spirit realm and led him outside. Jesus transported a whole boat with His disciples in it to the other side of the sea after He came walking to them on the water.

I know a man in South Africa that was given instructions by the Lord to walk to Cape Town and pray for a man. The problem was that he lived in Johannesburg, which was hundreds of miles away. As he began walking, he recalls being on the side of the highway and cars were coming up behind him and not gaining on him. He began passing cars like lightning as if he were a super hero walking at a normal pace. He states that he had only been on the road fifteen minutes when he saw a sign that said "Welcome to Cape Town." This man walked 785 miles from Johannesburg to Cape Town, South Africa in 15 minutes! That's a supernatural highway!

Supernatural transportation or translocation comes through union with God, birthed from a holy desperation to know the limitless measures of His Kingdom. Ian Clayton, a good friend of mine, has reported this happening to him for some 12 to 15 years now, and he has kept it very quiet. Ian has always hungered for physical evidence of his transportation experiences.

White Clouds and Fire Tunnels

After being in prolonged periods of communion with the Lord, Ian said there would come a tunnel of fire and a white cloud of Glory that would appear and shift him into the spirit realm. In this process, Ian has learned to recognize signs that would indicate he was about to take a trip. He has never looked back to see if he has physically gone, but there have been many strong evidences that he had.

One time Ian reported being transported to India where there was a man in a desert region talking with him, wanting to know about the Kingdom. He was an old shaman that had wanted to know God, and Ian ministered to him for over an hour. On the way back from his encounter, as he was about to go through the portal of fire, Ian reached down to pick up a handful of sand to take it back with him, and the Lord spoke to him: "If you take that back, you will never go again." Ian dropped the sand.

Ian states that these trips develop into stages of intensity when the portal of fire opens up. Recently, he had been transported to an eastern country where there was a lot of gunfire going on. There he saw a mother and three children in a house that were terrified in their circumstances. Ian states that a supernatural door had opened up to them in the wall and he was able to speak in a language he had never studied.

Ian spoke to the woman and said, "I've come to help you."

The woman looked at Ian and asked, "Who sent you?"

Ian responded in the foreign language, "God has sent me. Come quickly." From the look on the woman's face, she obviously understood him. The woman and children followed Ian through the supernatural door that lead down to passageways and to a large wall. He lifted the three children up over the wall with the mother and as he jumped to lift himself over the wall, his hands slipped off the concrete on top of the wall, scraping his chest as he fell to the pavement below.

When Ian hit the pavement he found himself back in his bedroom, bent over on the floor and holding his chest in pain. Baffled by the whole experience Ian went to bed. In the morning as he stood up, he saw large black and blue scrape marks and bruises across his chest. He had physical evidence of the encounter that occurred the night before. Ian states that these experiences are normal and accessible in the realm of the spirit and that he has had many over the past years.

John Paul Jackson of Streams Ministries had an encounter while preaching in Ireland. He had been on the road with Bob Jones and had gotten very ill, so much so that he had to stay back in the hotel for lack of strength. While lying on his bed, he saw an old, apparently South American man standing next to him. He thought, "I must be going to die; I'm hallucinating." John Paul prayed, "Lord, if this man is from You, please have him put his hand on my body and pray for me to recover." Immediately, the man did just that, and John Paul was overcome by the power of God that filled his whole body.

John Paul asked the man, "Where did you come from?"

He stated, "I was praying that God would use me one more time in my old age as He did in the past, and I found myself here with you." After a short period of time, the man disappeared.

Bob Jones recently told me that while praying in the Spirit he was visited by a man dressed in an orange robe. Bob described the man as a dark-skinned holy man from India. The man told Bob his name was Sundar Singh. Bob had never heard of this man before, but he is well known to many in the world as a modern mystic who disappeared in the Himalayan Mountains. As Sundar was leaving, he reached over to Bob and hugged him. This man was physical! He had stepped out of the great cloud of witnesses in Hebrews 12 and materialized in front of Bob. We think we have it all figured out in the western world, but I tell you that we are babes concerning the mysteries of the Spirit realm.

The apostle Paul was visited in the night by a *"man from Macedonia"* asking him to come and help him with the work of the Lord there (see Acts 16:9).

Jan Jansen, my wife, has been transported or translated several times. She had one profound experience where she was taken from our sofa to Africa.

People think that everything that happens when you are asleep is a dream, but this is not the case. God often waits to "use us" in atypical ways when we are asleep or falling asleep because when we are awake we are so busy and preoccupied that we are not yielded to what He wants to do in us and through us. Often when you feel sleepy or tired when you normally wouldn't, God wants to speak to you or use you while you are asleep or resting. Bob Jones has said that when he is feeling unusually tired in the middle of the day or at a time he wouldn't normally feel sleepy, he eagerly allows himself to fall asleep because he knows he is going to have an encounter.

Jan was feeling unusually sleepy and tired one afternoon, so although she had much to do, she lay down on the sofa and began to fall asleep. Before she was even completely asleep, suddenly she felt herself being taken by the Spirit. She found herself walking on very hot sand, with a hot sun beating down on her. As she began to look around she saw many people, all dark-skinned. She doesn't know why she was sure she was in Africa, but she states that in her spirit she just knew. She knew it was not a dream because everything she sensed in her five senses was real, not symbolic as in a dream. She felt the heat, sensed the dry air, felt the wind, and smelled the aromas.

She wasn't sure why she was there, but she continued to walk. Although there were large crowds of people there, her eyes were immediately drawn to one family. They were sitting on what appeared to be an old wagon bed. It was wood and had axles on it where wheels used to be. There was a mother, a father, and three children. It was apparent that the mother was blind, as was one of the children. The mother was also very pregnant. Compassion welled up in her as she approached the family. They seemed apprehensive and frightened of her as she obviously looked very different from the rest of the locals there.

She said she was actually reluctant to speak with them, not knowing if they would even understand her. But she walked over to the father and asked, "Do you know God?" She could tell they were afraid of religious persecution because as she said this they all began to look around to see if anyone had heard. They ducked their heads and refused to look at her. She said, "It's OK. I am a Christian." They nodded, and she knew that they were too, but not openly. Perhaps it was a Muslim country and Christians were persecuted there. But she knew this family had been praying for God to send them help.

Jan said she then asked the mother why she was blind—had she been born blind, or become blind later in life? She also asked about the child. They did not answer and continued to be afraid someone would hear. Jan said she felt it was not necessary to ask them any more questions, but just knew if she extended her hand toward them, they would be healed and the blindness would be gone. So she simply asked if she could pray for them; they nodded "yes," and she put her hands on the mother and child. Suddenly a bolt of lightning hit her and the entire family, and the power of God began to surge through them all.

Then, as quickly as she was transported or translated *to* Africa, she was back on the couch again, still feeling the electric bolt surging through her body. She said she shook violently for at least 20 minutes after the experience. She was never able to see what happened or if the family was healed and set free, but she knew in her spirit that they were.

Ian Clayton was transported to a jail cell in China where there were five men who were being tortured for their faith by communist soldiers. These soldiers were screaming at Ian and the men for extended periods of time. Finally, the soldiers threw several men down to the ground and onto wooden crosses and proceeded to crucify them. Ian watched as they drove nails into their hands and listened to their pleas for mercy and screams of agony. Two men approached Ian and wrestled him to the ground. They fought with Ian and positioned him on the cross as they had the other men. Ian said he felt the excruciating pain in his body as the nails went through his hands and into the wood and that all he could do was go "into himself" as he put it. As he did, he found himself back in his bed. When Ian woke in the morning, his hands actually had wounds in them from the encounter the night before.

We're Not Weird, They Are

It is time to settle it. The spirit realm is the real realm. If we can learn to agree with the Lord in the spirit, we will go higher in God than any other generation before us. Supernatural experiences like this are normal to the believer; however, people throughout history have been persecuted and locked up, and others have been looked down upon for having encounters like these. Bob Jones told me one time, "We're not the weird ones—they are!" Supernatural encounters are normal behavior to the believer.

I have a friend who was recently in a service speaking about heavenly transportations when, in the very act of preaching and raising his hands, he found himself on a crowded elevator surrounded by Chinese people. As he got off the elevator and walked into the lobby, he went outside and looked up and down the city streets and noticed that all of the signs were in Chinese. God had transported him to China. He prayed with a group of people there and exchanged contact information. Weeks later, he received a letter from them thanking him for coming and encouraging them.

David Hogan, a ministry friend of mine, was transported to a safe location after he had been held hostage by military guerillas in Mexico for preaching the Gospel. They were going to kill him but decided at the last moment to let him leave on his motorcycle. As he was racing to get away from the situation, his bike came to a steep cliff that he remembered going over. Moments later he supernaturally found himself safe below in front of a market on his bike.

Transportations are to be a normal part of the believer's life. These supernatural highways are accessible to all who believe. God designed Adam to walk and move in this system, and He has not changed His protocol or His mind. As mentioned earlier Adam was created a duel-dimensional man with access to both the spirit world and the natural dimension without limit. Adam walked in union and fellowship with God and understood the secrets of creation. Adam listened to the Lord with fascination as the Lord explained to him how all things were created. God held nothing back with His newly created son. Adam, too, was given the ability to create and bring forth, and God took great delight in watching to see what Adam would create.

Heavenly Substance

Roland Buck tells a story in his book *Angels on Assignment.* He was at his desk preparing for a meeting at church when he laid his head on his Bible to pray for the evening service. Instantly, he was standing in Heaven and was both shown and given a parchment by an angel with 120 specific events that were to take place. He recalls the experience as a real-to-life event so much so that as he was coming back into the natural realm he saw himself from above still sitting at his chair with his head down in prayer. As he came to himself after the encounter, he found that he still had the parchment with the 120 events on it clutched in his hand. He brought his wife and staff members in to see it, and it was with them for several days until the parchment slowly began to evaporate and then finally disappear.

Angels with Rubies

In the summer of 2006, the Lord woke me up to pray at 4:00 A.M. As I was in my chair praying, suddenly standing before me was the Spirit of Wisdom. In this encounter she (female) stood before me telling me how she was a master builder in the beginning with God creating all things. She quoted from Proverbs 8 and said than to get wisdom was better that gold or rubies, and that those who sought her early would find her. Here I

Ruby Stone

was in my chair at four in the morning having a 45-minute encounter with the Spirit of Wisdom.

As she finished, the Spirits of Council and Might stood in front of me, each with parchments of lambskin about four feet in length with writing on both sides. They proceeded to cause me to eat the scrolls of destiny. At the close of this encounter, another angel stood in front of me. I'd seen this angel before. This angel had been bringing large gemstones of 50 carats in size to the Pacific Northwest over the past season. Now this angel was standing in front of me holding a 50-carat ruby. In the vision the angel gave it to me, hand to hand. The next day I was off to a meeting in Washington state with some of my Glory friends. This angel showed up in the meeting with the 50-carat ruby and physically handed it to a friend of mine who was directed by the Lord to give it to me. This all came in a heavenly encounter the day before.

I personally know of intercessors who have gone to the treasure room in Heaven and have brought back jewelry and garments. These things aren't talked about much, but have been the experience of many in Church history, stemming from intimacy and communion with the Lord Jesus. Jesus took Peter, James, and John up on the mountain of transfiguration in Mark 9:2, and the environment and raiment of Jesus was transformed in front of them. Not only that, but they encountered Moses and Elijah there as well. Is this normal? According to Jesus it is!

Spirit Travel

In spirit travel there is a special faith, anointing, and protection placed around the individual so that person can perform what the Lord is leading him or her to do. When an out-of-the-body experience takes place, the person's spirit literally leaves the physical body and travels in the spirit world by the Spirit of the Lord. The surrounding environment appears different as that person is seeing in the spirit and not the natural. The Lord directs our eyes to see what He wants us to see. Ezekiel had many experiences like this:

So the Spirit lifted me up and took me away...(Ezekiel 3:14).

He [the Spirit of the Lord] *stretched out the form of a hand and caught me by a lock of my head...* (Ezekiel 8:1-3).

...the Spirit lifted me up and brought me... (Ezekiel 11:1).

The hand of the Lord was upon me, and He brought me out by the Spirit of the Lord and set me down... (Ezekiel 37:1).

And the Spirit lifted me up and brought me... (Ezekiel 43:5).

Interior Graces of Prayer

The out-workings of the miraculous in transportations and heavenly encounters are a wonder and are awesome in themselves. But these spiritual dimensions are only possible through the outer workings of the *interior graces* of prayer. Transformation of the mind and the spirit of people through communion with God is crucial. In order for the outward to manifest the Kingdom of God, there needs to be the complete possessing of the inward parts of people. This comes about not by understanding or by reason, but rather by self-abandonment and the complete overtaking of the Holy Spirit in an individual's life. Deep prayer and communion with God are the catalyst for Heaven to open up and for the experience of supernatural encounters.

Angels That Assist

Angels are most often involved in supernatural encounters, acting as agents between God and humans. Often they will bring instructions and direction in these experiences. Angels are mighty and powerful heavenly beings. They are the messengers of God. Their main duty is to worship God and also to see that the instructions of God are carried out. They patrol the earth. They help, protect, and minister to God's people. They carry out most of the activities between Heaven and the believers, and sometimes they even appear to unbelievers. They are very strong, intelligent, obedient, and swift. They can reach any part of the universe in seconds. One angel can also kill hundreds of thousands of human beings in just one night, as we will soon see.

Before we see some of their activities and how they can aid our warfare, let's understand what Jesus was saying in the text of Matthew 26:47-56. As Jesus was coming up from Gethsemane with his disciples, they met Judas who had come with a division of armed soldiers to arrest him. Immediately, Jesus identified himself—*"I am He"*—and they all fell to the ground (see John 18:6). Thereafter, He willingly submitted Himself to them. But Peter did not want to see this happen. He immediately drew his sword and chopped off the ear of the high priest's servant. Jesus reacted by telling Peter to put away his sword, that if He (Jesus) wanted protection then He could have requested His Father to send thousands of angels to fight for Him. But it was unnecessary because it was time to accomplish what He came to the earth to do—to die for the sins of the world.

In fact, the King James Version puts it this way: *"Thinkest thou that I cannot now pray to My Father, and He shall presently give Me more than twelve legions of angels"* (Matt. 26:53 KJV). A legion is about 6,000 soldiers, so 12 legions will be 72,000 soldiers. So Jesus was saying that if He wanted He could have asked God to give Him 72,000 battle-ready angels to defend and fight for Him.

Now, do you know the implication of this? If one angel could kill as many as 185,000 Assyrian troops in just one night, then 72,000 angels would be able to kill 13,320,000,000 people in this same time—one night (see 2 Kings 19:35). And tell me, what was the population of the world then? How many people would remain? But Jesus did not take that option because it was His time—it was the will of God that He be sacrificed for the redemption of humankind.

But our interest here is that Jesus was telling us that we have the possibility of asking the Father to send angels for the protection of His people and that God would do that instantly. Great! Now you will ask yourself, does the Church appreciate this great truth? But before we go into the Scriptures and personal testimonies, I want to emphasize here that Jesus said that He could have prayed to the Father to send the angels. Note that He would not pray to the angels directly. It is the Father that will send the angels. But they will come to minister, serve, help, protect, defend, and fight for us. Praise God!

Let's first see where angels fought for the people of God in the Bible. At one time in the life of the people of Israel, the enemy threatened them with imminent attack. Sennacherib had fought and conquered Israel. Israel paid Sennacherib tribute of tons of gold and silver. They stripped the gold from temple of the Lord to meet this demand by King Sennacherib of Assyria, yet he was not satisfied. He insulted the Israelites, their king, Hezekiah, and even their God. Sennacherib threatened to not just defeat them in battle again, but to humiliate and relocate Israel from their land.

Hezekiah, the king of Israel, heard all the threats of the king of Assyria, tore his clothes, wore sackcloth, and went into the Temple of the Lord to pray. He spread out the letter of threats the king of Assyria had sent to him. After he prayed, God answered and assured him that He would fight for His people. And what happened? That same night God sent His angel to battle and humiliate the enemies of Israel. Just one angel defeated the soldiers and their commander. King Sennacherib ran home in disgrace.

That night the angel of Lord went out to the Assyrian camp and killed 185,000 Assyrian soldiers. When the surviving Assyrians woke up the next morning, they found corpses everywhere. Then King Sennacherib of Assyria broke camp and retuned to his own land. He went home to his capital of Nineveh and stayed there (2 Kings 19:35-36 NLT).

The angel killed 185,000 soldiers, disorganized the surviving ones, and sent their commander-in-chief scampering for safety. This is exactly what happens when God sends His angels to fight our battles. It is always devastating. The prayer warriors and in fact all Christians must learn and always apply this strategy—involving the heavenly angels in our warfare. Demons, witches, and even satan can sometimes trick you, but they always run at the sight of the angels of God. And you know, these heavenly warriors, when coming for battle, come on horses and chariots of fire with their flaming swords in their hands. Who will see such fearful sight and not run away? Always ask God to send His mighty angels to fight for you when you are in warfare with the kingdom of darkness.

Daniel also understood the operations of the angels. He knew that God could shut the mouths of lions. Just read this account:

So at last the king gave orders for Daniel to be arrested and thrown into the den of lions. The king said to him, "May your God, whom you serve so faithfully, rescue you." A stone was brought and placed over the mouth of the den. The king sealed the stone with his own royal seal and the seals of his nobles, so that no one could rescue Daniel. Then the king returned to his palace and spent the night fasting. He refused his usual entertainment and couldn't sleep at all that night. Very early the next morning, the king got up and hurried out to the lions' den. When he got there, he called out in anguish, "Daniel, servant of the living God! Was your God, whom you serve so faithfully, able to rescue you from the lions?" Daniel answered, "Long live the king!

My God sent His angel to shut the lions' mouths so that they would not hurt me" (Daniel 6:16-22 NLT).

Praise God! He sent His angel to shut the mouths of lions. One angel shut the mouths of many lions. That is just how powerful angels are. You may not need many. Just one is enough to silence all your enemies.

I am not surprised that Daniel easily understood that it was only an angel that could close the mouths of those voracious beasts in that cave. He had so many encounters with heavenly beings, so he knew their operations. He had the rare privilege of knowing that the prayer of a believer has the power to cause so many cosmic reactions amongst the elite beings in the spiritual realm. Let's read more of the insights he was privileged to know:

He replied, "Do you know why I have come? Soon I must return to fight against the spirit prince of the kingdom of Persia, and after that the spirit prince of the kingdom of Greece will come. Meanwhile, I will tell you what is written in the Book of Truth. (No one helps me against these spirit princes except Michael, your spirit prince)" (Daniel 10:20-21 NLT).

Daniel triggered these struggles among these mighty spirit beings through his persistent prayers. And the struggle is for the deliverance and well-being of the children of God—Israel. We will understand this better if God opens our eyes to see some of the activities of the host of Heaven on our behalf, especially when we pray or run into a dangerous situation.

David knew how the angels fight for God's people. Look at some of his prayers and statements:

Let those be ashamed and dishonored who seek my life; let those be turned back and humiliated who devise evil

*against me. Let them be like chaff before the wind, with
the angel of the Lord driving them on. Let their way be
dark and slippery, with the angel of the Lord pursuing
them* (Psalm 35:4-6).

*The Angel of the Lord encamps around those who fear
Him [who revere and worship Him with awe] and each
of them He delivers* (Psalm 34:7 AMP).

We can go on and on. The activities of the angels are everywhere
in the Bible from Genesis to Revelation. We just referred to few places
where they fought on behalf of the children of God. The prayer warriors
and indeed all Christians should take advantage of this great weapon
that God has graciously made available to us.

Endnote

1. *Merriam-Webster Online Dictionary,* s.v. "Image," www
.merriam-webster.com/dictionary/image (accessed March 24, 2009).

CHAPTER 10

UNHOLY PATHWAYS
OF THE OCCULT

In the next few pages I want to share with you some of the realities that are known to happen in the occult. In our day there are those like David Blaine and Chris Angel in the spotlight on television, glorifying the practice of the magic arts. There are also books and movies, like *Harry Potter,* that glorify sorcery and wizardry, and it's all aimed at pulling children into this world. Many are being swept away by the marvels of their craft. Believe me, these individuals are tame in comparison to those that are after the higher levels of power in satanism. Just as there is the true and the genuine, there is also the false. The occult is deep; it is one of the oldest practices known to humanity. These dark spiritual pathways of incantations and black magic were clearly taught to humans by fallen angels, who revealed supernatural knowledge of how to move in dark pathways.

In the following chapters, I want to reveal details and accounts of occult activity, not as a means of glorifying it, but rather to reveal the hidden design and nature of humanity as God-created supernatural beings. If the fallen, unregenerate person can move with powerful demonstrations in dark supernatural ability, what do we as blood-bought, Spirit-filled believers have access to by the Holy Spirit of God? (Note that the information you are about to read is somewhat graphic and may challenge some of your western mindsets and theology.)

Shape-shifters and Transcended Physics

Dave Bryant tells the following story about his experience:

> It was in mid-October of 1997. We had been ministering deliverance and inner healing to Deborah, a woman who had come out of deep, generational occult involvement in the church of satan. Most of her family members were still involved in heavy occult activities of various kinds. One of her sisters had left the church of satan in preference for what she believed to be a more pure source of evil—a *were*-cult (where we get the word "werewolf") based in New Mexico. Were-cults—like their aquatic *mere*-cult or "mermaid" counterparts—are based on establishing human partnerships with certain kinds of evil spirits. These spirits have powers to manipulate physical realities and transcend the natural laws of physical matter which we consider to be normal.
>
> While these apparent contradictions to established laws of science are challenging for our "spiritually neutered," rationalistic western minds, they are certainly well-documented in Scripture. The entire sphere of the "miraculous" is dubbed such based on an established experience that contradicts our narrow understanding of the laws that govern the physical realm. The Scriptural accounts of animals talking, axe heads floating on water,

men possessed by super-human powers carrying off the fortified gates of an entire city, prophets taking trips in the spirit world, or angels appearing out of nowhere, taking on a physical form and then engaging in physical activities (such as eating and drinking)—all are such examples of transcended physics.

Scripture also records the involvement of "incubus" spirits making their bid to defile the human race and corrupt humankind's lineage (see Gen. 6:1-7). This was a diabolical attempt to prevent the "seed of woman" from ever bruising satan's head and fulfilling the Edenic prophecy of Genesis 3:15. In these and similar instances, the spirits involved were fallen, evil spirits who still retained these special powers, but now employed them in service to satan rather than to Christ, the Lord of Hosts. These spirits are behind the pervasive stories, legends, and cultural beliefs of were- and mere-beasts (werewolves and mermaids).

Deborah had recounted for us numerous stories of such spirits in her family and their past occult involvements, and had warned us that her sister was a "serious player" in the realm of such "shape-shifters." As the high season of occult celebration—Halloween—ticked by that year, the spiritual climate in our area reached a feverishly high boiling point in the conflict between good and evil. Deborah had warned us that things were heating up in the spirit world and that the occult leaders of various groups were joining forces for a "power convergence" in our area.

We were keeping Deborah in our home and had begun to take more serious precautions as the spiritual energy levels were escalating. I had taken Deborah to our local Wal-Mart along with our three teenage sons to pick up a few essentials that day. We knew that she was under significant spiritual pressure, but it was midday and the trip would be a quick one. Since I was in a hurry to get back home, I was in no mood to stop by the pet section to "fish watch," but I thought it would be a fine distraction for Deborah and the boys while I picked up the few items on my shopping list.

I left them there in the pet section for all of five minutes, but returned to find the boys watching fish alone, with no idea where Deborah had gone. Hurrying from aisle to aisle in a frantic search for Deborah, I passed one of our staff couples near the entrance to the garden section. Too busy to visit, I asked if they had seen Deborah recently. They had, they admitted, but she was running down the shampoo aisle and acted like she was really scared. Thanking them, the boys and I headed for the parking lot, assuming that she may have run out of the store to escape whomever (or *whatever*) had frightened her. Near the front entrance, she joined us from her hiding place, and we ran for the car. Although unwilling to speak about it in the presence of the boys, she confided in Cheryl and I when back in the safety of our home again.

She told us that Zena, her sister, was in town for the occultic power convergence and that they had conjured certain powerful were-spirits to assist them in their evil schemes against us. She had seen one of these "transmuter" spirits in the store, and the sheer power of evil that it emitted had nearly overcome her. Just as she sensed the powerful presence of evil, it had emerged from the garden section, looking like an old woman bent over an empty shopping cart. Then it looked up at her, and she recognized the unmistakable characteristics of their kind. It looked very old, too old to be human, with hollow, empty white eyes, hair that looked like old straw from a weathered scarecrow, boney fingers, and reddish-black skin that looked and smelled like charred flesh.

"Anything else you can think of, Deborah?" I asked.

"Well, it had their kind of legs," she said.

"Their kind of legs?" I questioned. She explained that, for some reason, transmuter spirits that materialized *outside* a host almost always had knee joints that bent the wrong direction, like a chicken's legs.

"Hmmm," I mused, mainly to myself, as I thought of the depiction of the aliens that took on human forms in the 90s movie *The Arrival*. "Maybe somebody knows more than they're letting on in Hollywood," I thought.

We prayed together briefly, reminding Deborah that God's power was greater than *all* the power of the devil and that Jesus' perfect love casts out all fear. Then I retired to the front room to sit down in my "thinking chair" and ponder the whole bizarre situation. I wondered how much was true. Obviously, she had seen something and was convinced that it was extremely evil and that it was coming for her. She seemed very confident of her information and dead certain of the details. She had done what anyone would have done—she had fled for her life. But could all this mind-bending stuff about transmuter spirits and shape-shifters be true? Were troubled people having their fragile emotions and twisted imaginations stirred by Hollywood producers, or were Hollywood producers making films based on "deeper truths" that they were somehow privy to?

"Lord Jesus," I prayed, "Your Word says that truth is established by the witness of two or more testimonies of agreement, so please—if this is true, and it's important for us to know about—*please* let there be another confirming witness of some kind."

That's when the doorbell rang.

At the door stood my good friend, Pat. He was a long-term staff member at the Church of Glad Tidings and a man whose judgment I had always trusted. A former soldier, he was tough, street-smart, and not afraid of anything...at least nothing in our world. When I saw him, I knew something was desperately wrong. He was ashen white and looked as if he was very sick and about to faint. I invited him in, asking what was wrong and if his wife was with him. He assured me that something was bad wrong, but that he had taken his wife home and didn't want her to be involved in the situation. "What situation, Patrick?" I asked.

He asked, "First of all, did you ever find Deborah?" When I said that I had reconnected with her just after seeing him at the store and that she was resting upstairs, he wanted to know if she was alright or if she had seen something evil in Wal-Mart.

"She's OK, Pat, but why would you ask a weird question like that?"

"Well," he stammered uncomfortably, "I saw something very evil in Wal-Mart, and I somehow knew that she had seen it, too."

"What about your wife? Did she see it?" I asked.

"No! She was looking at the flowers. When I saw it, I was paralyzed with fear, and I couldn't move. I felt really sick, like I might even die if it looked at me again. I tried to pray, but I couldn't seem to move my lips or make any noise. I asked Jesus to help me in my heart, and then it just disappeared. So I left our shopping cart right where it was, grabbed my wife, and ran to the car. I told her that I thought I knew what had scared Deborah and that I had to talk to you about it right away, so I dropped her off at the house and came straight over here."

"Hmmm. Well, let's hear about it. What exactly did you see?"

"Well, at first I thought it was a really old lady, leaning over a cart in the garden section. When I tried to get around her, I smelled a putrefying odor, like rotten meat, and I thought I was going to puke. Then she turned to look at me, and I nearly passed out. She looked a bazillion years old, and her eyes were white like the zombies on a horror flick. She didn't have real hair. It was just like rotten straw or something, and her whole body had been burned horrifically. She looked like she had been burned to death and then she got resurrected or something. She still smelled like rotten meat, and whatever it was, she was really, really evil!"

He drank his ice water and wiped the sweat off his forehead, searching my gaze as if desperate to convince me that he was sane and that his story could be trusted. I looked into his eyes for a very long minute, praying in my spirit and struggling to keep my own equilibrium.

"And her legs?" I prodded gently.

"Huh?" He mumbled as his tortured mind looked for reasonable words.

"Did you see her legs, Patrick? If you did, it's important that you tell me exactly what you think you saw. Did you happen to see her legs?"

He suddenly looked relieved and slumped in his chair, heaving a big sigh. "So she *did* see it, didn't she? That's why you're asking about its legs. She saw that it had its knee caps on backwards, didn't she?"

"Knee caps on backwards?" I dummied up.

"Yeah. Like chicken's legs. They bent the wrong way, just like the aliens in *The Arrival*!"

Now it was time for me to sigh. "Thank you, Jesus, for confirming something as 'unbelievable' as this with such unmistakable clarity," I prayed under my breath.

"Yeah, Patrick. Deborah saw the same thing, and if it helps put your poor mind at ease a little, she described it *exactly* the same way! The same features—she even used some of the identical phrases that you used to describe its hair, skin, eyes, and legs."

"So you don't think I'm crazy, then?"

"Don't jump to such rash conclusions, Patrick. I just said Deborah saw the same thing. That's way different from giving you a clean bill of mental health!"

We laughed together and then prayed, thanking the Lord for His great power available to us through the Holy Spirit and for His mighty warring angels who are sent to serve us who are the heirs of His salvation. We wondered if this would be a one-time incident, or if it was a precursor to what lay ahead.

Just a few days later, Deborah told us that Zena and her friends were "casing" our house with frequent drive-bys. She said that some were in a black limo, but that Zena was driving a red convertible mustang. Two days later, we received a concern call from one of our neighbors, who often watched our house for us when we were traveling. "Grandma," as we called her, was concerned that people were spying on us. She had seen both the black limo and the red convertible numerous times over the three previous days—at all hours of the day and night—driving by our house slowly, often parking at the curb for a while before moving on. "Watch out for Zena," Deborah warned. "They're definitely up to something!"

We prayed together for God's protection and for His love to *"cast out fear"* (see 1 John 4:18). Then I headed for Glad Tidings for another exciting day at the office.

Just before I left to return home that afternoon, I was spending some time in prayer. I had instructed my secretary to hold all calls and to not allow any disruptions except in the case of an extreme emergency. So when the intercom crackled, "Dave, Pat is at your door and he really needs to talk to you right away!" I knew there was a significant problem. Opening my office door, I saw that same frantic look on my friend's face that I had seen following the Wal-Mart "transmuter" appearance. This time, it was Zena herself.

Pat explained that he was busy around the campus when he noticed a red convertible Mustang stopped in the parking lot near our Junior Junction Daycare facility. He had noticed it for several reasons. First, it was not parked in one of the many available striped parking stalls, but had merely stopped in the drive thoroughfare that continued on through the campus. Secondly, the convertible top was down, even though the late October afternoon would have dictated otherwise for most California drivers. Thirdly, the woman seemed to be looking intently at the day care facility, as if she was confused or concerned. He watched for a few seconds, and then continued on with his activities. But when he returned five minutes later and saw that the car and its driver hadn't moved, he headed over to see if he could be of any assistance. Approaching the car from the rear on the driver's side, he could only see the driver's long blonde hair.

"Excuse me, Ma'am. Can I help you with anything?" Pat asked in his usual cheerful way.

"I was shocked when I heard her begin to snarl at me, and I wondered if that awful noise could possibly be coming from the blonde woman. Then she turned around, and her snout was huge!"

"She had a big nose?" I suggested.

"It wasn't a nose, Dave. She had a snout!" Not yet connecting all the dots in the picture, and still trying to collect accurate information, I asked him if he thought she needed a cosmetic surgery to correct her problem.

"Surgery couldn't correct her problem, Dave. She needed her whole face removed! It wasn't a woman, Dave. It was a wolf's head on a woman's body!"

"Zena!" I whispered under my breath. She had visited us and brought her shape-shifting spirit friends with her.

We have experienced the reality of "transcended physics" on a number of occasions in our ministry as we have sought to fulfill the mandate of Isaiah 61:1-7 to release captives from their prison-houses of darkness. To the stories recounted above we could add many others. There have been instances of corporal bodies being pulled through physical structures, as was the case when evil spirits "pulled" Deborah's legs through the firewall of our Chevy van all the way up to her knees. When we rebuked them in Jesus' name, Deborah was miraculously pulled back into her seat with *no harm* done to either her legs or to the firewall of our van! Deborah's legs went through the area below the dash, above the floorboard of the van. She was being physically pulled against her will into the spirit world. She was screaming, "I am a natural person and you can not do this to me." All the while she was disappearing through the floorboard of the van. Finally it broke and she returned to the original position in her car seat. Of course I was rebuking hell and praying in tongues frantically.

These stories are never questioned in many of the nations of the world that hold a more spiritual worldview than the "enlightened" nations of the West. They are criticized as sensational and unreasonable by the great majority of the pastors and spiritual leaders in the west. While we "amen" the stories of Jesus walking on the water or passing through the walls of buildings while in fully-physical form after His resurrection, why are we so quick to say, "That's impossible" at hearing of similarly miraculous accounts today? These clear examples of the "higher laws" of the spirit world should pave the way for any honest minds to admit to the reality of spiritually transcended physics being an expected reality in our day. Once there, the details are just that—*details*. Yet despite the frequent biblical examples of transcended physics, the traditions of western Christendom have been distorted by unabashed skepticism and a pervasive reliance on a rationalistic worldview to the point that such accounts are nearly always written off—even by "Bible-believing spiritual leaders"—as somewhere between fanciful imagination and blatant heresy. And because the church has largely relegated itself to the status of the "unbelievers" in this transcendent realm, many spiritually famished souls have found higher experiences in the dark realms of the occult.[1]

Satanists Enter My Room

In 2005, the Lord sent me to Seattle, Washington, to release a word specifically for the Pacific Northwest. After ministering the first evening, I released the word to the four winds over the three major cities there—Tacoma, Seattle, and Olympia. That night I had some of the most horrific dreams I had ever experienced. As I was coming out of sleep early in the morning, I awoke to three men standing in my hotel room. They were tall and skinny, wearing pinstriped suits and top hats, and looked like bowling pins next to one another. I sat up in bed and wiped my eyes only to have them disappear in front of me.

I immediately rang Jan and asked if she and the kids were OK. She said she was fine and proceeded to tell me she was going to the store with her friend. I told her to be very careful today and kept the experience to myself. I hung up the phone and got ready for the day. I rang her back an hour later to ask her a question and a strange woman answered the phone and said in a sheepish voice, "Hello." I asked for Jan and the woman said, "Now Mr. Jansen, don't be alarmed. Your wife was in a serious car accident, but we think she is going to be alright."

Jan and our friend Mary were driving to the grocery store. It was the middle of the morning so traffic was very light. They had pulled into a convenience store and were trying to cross over the three-lane street at an intersection. Jan states she looked both ways at least twice, if not three times. She crossed the street without hesitation, and before she knew what was happening, a car hit her very hard in the passenger door. The woman driving that car had not seen Jan, nor had Jan seen her. Thankfully, Jan was not seriously injured, but Mary had a fractured pelvis. God healed her in record time, but as the smoke cleared from this whole event, Jan was reminded of a dream she had about a week before. She was in a hospital gown and the back of her gown was open, leaving her exposed. In the dream, she was unable to see and kept repeating, "I can't see, I can't see." She was unable to interpret the dream and wrote it off as a "pizza dream," but this accident was clearly an attack of the enemy and the dream was a warning. The word *occult* means *hidden*. She literally was unable to see the car that was about to hit her as it was obscured from her view by a demonic force.

Supernatural Pathways of Darkness

Pastor Gabriel N. Agbo is an Assembly of God preacher in Nigeria. Being in Nigeria, Pastor Gabriel has had many dealings with witches, satanists, and occultism, and the following are personal writings and accounts of his ministry in Africa:

> We've experienced many dealings with people moving in supernatural pathways of darkness called trans-relocation. Trans-relocation is the ability to move from one place (or realm) to another through supernatural means. This ability is obtainable both in the Kingdom of God as well as the satanic kingdom of darkness, while it is consciously induced for evil purposes in the dark kingdom. It is only initiated and executed by the Holy Spirit in God's Kingdom to achieve divine purposes. A Christian (or believer) is not permitted to seek to trans-relocate (move) from one place to another beyond the natural means. Any conscientious effort to trans-relocate is not acceptable in Christianity. Its attempt instantly leads to occultism, and satan is at the head of all occult practices. Let's look at this phenomenon in the kingdom of darkness.[2]

The Kingdom of Darkness

It is a very common practice in the satanic kingdom to use demonic means to be able to move from one place to another. You see this practice in witchcraft, occultism, and in the false religions. It is often used by agents of darkness for various purposes which include attending demonic meetings and going to execute evil assignments.

In fact, almost all witches, advanced occultists, and their counterparts in false religions have this demonic ability. Remember that it is the same spirit—satan—that is working in them. For them to be efficient, they must be able to move supernaturally from one location to another. I have elsewhere talked about a man I know who travels abroad by going into a coffin placed in his "secret" room. I also talked about a blind native doctor (occultist) that I also know very well who has the ability to go into the water and stay for months in the marine kingdom. He is a very strong agent of that dark kingdom.

There are others who vanish when faced with any serious danger. They wear amulets (rings, waistbands, handkerchiefs, necklaces, et cetera) or make incisions on their bodies which give them the power to effectively remove themselves from any point of danger to a safer place, especially when the situation is a life-threatening one. You find these kinds of people in the military, police, among politicians, and many others in society.

There are a lot of high demonic manipulations going on in the kingdom of darkness. It is very true that the human agents of the satanic kingdom can travel to any part of the world and even to the planets without using any physical means of transportation.

Yes, agents of satan possess illegal supernatural powers, and it is common these days. This is also the reason why the church must rise from slumber.

I remember the confession of a former state deputy governor who is now a Christian in a fellowship which I attended in the '90s. He talked about his involvement in the occult world while seeking power and wealth. He narrated how he was practicing different high levels of occultism including disappearing, astral travels, et cetera. He said that one day he was traveling with his driver in his car and they came to a point where they bumped into a ditch. Immediately, he disappeared from the car and went to the house and waited for the driver. When the driver noticed that his boss has mysteriously disappeared from the car, he was confused and terribly afraid. He then drove home only to see the man waiting for him at home. The driver promptly resigned from the job.

This politician told us that he had a room in his house which only he entered. In that room, he had a very big magical rock hanging on a tiny thread tied across the room. He also said that he could travel to other continents by just entering into a coffin in that room. And this is just a glimpse of what goes on amongst our rulers. We must direct our prayers toward them for they are spiritual "gateways." When they serve satan the land is covenanted to satan, and when they serve God the land is equally covenanted to God. The Word of God says that when a righteous man is in authority, the people of the land will rejoice (see Prov. 29:2). The same goes for our companies and other organizations.[3]

Two Sources of Power

When Moses had Aaron throw down his rod it became a snake (see Ex. 7:10). The sorcerers also had rods that reduplicated the same sign, only notice that the Word says that Moses' *rod*, not snake, swallowed up their rods (see vs. 12)! The rod is symbolic of authority. The Bible says, *"They* [those who overcome] *will rule the nations with an iron rod..."* (Revelation 2:27 NLT). All those magicians had rods, but that day they went home "rod-less," for the authority of Moses swallowed up theirs. God is introducing us again to the supernatural dimension, but remember that lucifer said in Isaiah 14:14, *"I will...be **like** the Most High."* As with Moses, so it is with us that God's supernatural reality will overcome satan's counterfeit.

We as believers are dependent upon the Spirit of God, and witches are dependent upon demons and cycles of nature. For them, there are hindrances in performing certain rituals, based on the wrong time in the lunar cycle, the wrong pronunciation of a word in an incantation, or a lack of a preritual meditation. For us, the more child-like our faith becomes, the more we open up to our Father doing things in and through us that we hadn't even thought of before.

Witchcraft is another spirit the devil has released to destroy humankind and to battle the Church. This spirit is the most wicked of all spirits in the kingdom of darkness. All it wants to achieve is to destroy. You will always know its operations when you see manipulation, intimidation, and domination. It will always want to control no mater the cost. Witches are always afraid of midnight warriors. Though the strong ones will attempt to resist or even counter your attack, yet if you persist they will ultimately bow.

Who is a witch? A witch is a person, male or female, that is possessed by the spirit of witchcraft—a person that uses magic, charm, or spiritual powers for evil purposes

Witches normally meet in their covens (their spiritual meeting places) between 12 A.M. and 3 A.M. and sometimes beyond. Witches can turn into different forms when they go on operations or meetings. They can turn into birds, cats, owls, rats, cockroaches, vultures, snakes, et cetera. It depends on their assignments and situation. They usually turn into the forms that will help them gain entrance or achieve their particular objective in an operation. As I was putting this work together, I heard on the radio about a woman caught in the middle of the night by a trap set for the antelopes in the forest. When her captors asked her how she came into the trap, she confessed to being a witch. In Lagos, Nigeria, on many occasions large birds have fallen from the sky only to turn into human beings. I have even read a narrative by a very powerful, respected Pentecostal minister in Lagos telling how a witch was drawn down from the sky by their prayer force. She fell right there in their church premises and was pleading for mercy!

These things are not really strange to Africans or in some other places where the forces of darkness still reign. The dominant spirits you encounter in these places are marine spirits and the spirit of witchcraft, and these have also invaded the church. They are even moving into the house of God causing so much havoc to the believers and the Body of Christ. Their objective is to work against the plan of God. The church must wake up and battle this wicked spirit. We must break their strongholds and set the captives free.[4]

Powers in the Waters

There are also great powers and demonic activities from the waters. These we often refer to as the marine powers or spirits or "mere-spirits."

They are the spirits you see most often in the course of deliverance ministry in Africa, India, and other places. These marine spirits also manipulate and use humans. They operate mostly through physical and spiritual activities and sacrifices. People worship these demons for power, wealth, and protection. I know people who serve these demons that go into the water (rivers and seas) and stay for several months. These wicked spirits cause most of the accidents on our waterways and even roads. We must pray for their downfall and stop their activities against human beings and the work of God.

My good friend Todd Bentley was holding a crusade in Uganda, Africa. The team would pray over the crusade ground constantly, but no matter how hard they prayed, at the time of the crusade, dark clouds would come and threaten to shut the crusade down. Todd Bentley's father, Dave Bentley, and some of the other crusade members noticed that a witch doctor would come up out of the river at dusk and stand on the other side of the riverbank and curse the crusade. When he finished cursing the crusade he would go back under the river and stay there until the next day. When they dealt with it they received the breakthrough they needed and had a powerful crusade.

Once again, these stories are not meant to glorify satan or the realm of the demonic. They have been included only to reveal the hidden design and nature of humanity as supernatural beings. These stories cause us to understand that *anybody* can operate in the supernatural, but only blood-bought, Spirit-filled sons and daughters have the legal right to do so.

Endnotes

1. Dave and Cheryl Bryant, in conversation with the author (www.churchofgladtidings.com).

2. Pastor Gabriel N. Agabo, in conversation with the author (Assemblies of God, Nigeria).

3. Ibid.

4. Ibid.

[CHAPTER 11]

THE SPIRIT OF MAN

Reading the past few chapters I'm sure has been both challenging and exhilarating as we ponder the question: "Who are we?" Sages, philosophers, theologians, and curious people throughout the ages of time have asked this question. David asked that very question of God as he considered God's handiwork in creation:

> *What is man that You take thought of him, and the son of man that You care for him? Yet You have made him a little lower than God, and You crown him with glory and majesty! You make him to rule over the works of Your hands; You have put all things under his feet, all sheep and oxen, and also the beasts of the field, the birds of the heavens and the fish of the sea, whatever passes through the paths of the seas (Ps. 8:4-8).*

It is a good question and one that begs answers. "Why are we here? Where did we come from? How old are we?" Indeed, we live on a planet spinning in infinite space—why are we here? We'll seek answers to these questions, at least in part. Let's discover what the Bible has to say about these perplexing inquiries.

What Is Man?

We already know through Genesis 1:26-27 that we are made in the image and likeness of God. Not only do we have the same shape and form as God, but we also have similar faculties of mind, will, and emotion. Thus, we are like God in those respects. We are children of God, and like begets like. Essentially though, we are spirit. The Scriptures refer often to humans as spirit; this is the first truth we should grasp.

> For who among men knows the thoughts of a man except the spirit of the man which is in him? Even so the thoughts of God no one knows except the Spirit of God (1 Corinthians 2:11).

> The spirit of man is the lamp of the Lord, searching all the innermost parts of His being (Proverbs 20:27).

The next logical question is, "How long has your spirit been in existence?" Was your spirit created the day you were conceived on the earth or at the point of your spiritual birth?

Let me tell you, you are very old!

> ...who has saved us and called us with a holy calling, not according to our works, but according to His own purpose and grace which was given to us in Christ Jesus before time began (2 Timothy 1:9 NKJV).

God gave us a calling and purpose before we were born into this world and before the world was created—before time even! You were alive before the creation of the world. The gift of salvation and your calling and purpose was a gift from eternity. Even though we weren't yet born in the natural, Christ existed as the covenant head and representative of His people. We were in Him as members of Him, represented by Him, united to Him, and we were blessed in Him with all spiritual blessings.

> *Before I formed you in the womb I knew you, and before you were born I consecrated you; I have appointed you a prophet to the nations* (Jeremiah 1:5).

In the above verse, the Lord is telling Jeremiah that before he was even born into this world God had ordained him to be a prophet to the nations. This ordination of Jeremiah to be a prophet wasn't done in time, but in eternity.

Astounding Truth

One day, while in prayer, the Lord began to speak with me and give me revelation and understanding about the trial of Job. What I found out filled me with awe, and I would like to share what I learned with you.

In the first 37 chapters of the Book of Job, he complained about his lot in life and the great trial he was going through. Then God called him to account and asked:

> *Where were you when I laid the foundation of the earth? Tell Me, if you have understanding, who set its measurements?* ***Since you know.*** *Or who stretched the line on it? On what were its bases sunk? Or who laid its cornerstone, when the morning stars sang together and* ***all the sons of God shouted for joy*** (Job 38:4-7).

In other words, "Job, where were you when I created the world, when I did all these things? You know. These people, the sons of God, were there then and saw it all."

Then God continues, *"You know, for you were born then, and the number of your days is great"* (Job 38:21). God is not mocking Job here. Let's check out a few more versions of the Bible:

> *You must know, since you were born then! Or because you are so extremely old* (Job 38:21 AMP).

> *Surely you know, for you were already born! You have lived so many years* (Job 38:21 NIV).

> *But of course you know all this! For you were born before it was all created, and you are so very experienced* (Job 38:21 NLT).

These Scripture translations make clear that Job was one of the sons of God who shouted for joy when this world was created. Furthermore, he had great insight into God's handiwork in the formation of the earth in intricate detail. The wonder of it all is even greater when you realize that you were there too, as Job was. You were there when God created the world. We don't recall or remember because the details are lost—they fade and are veiled when we enter this life on earth and become clothed in mortal flesh.

Job at first told God that he wanted to die (see Job 6:8-9). God jogged his memory about the creation details he had seen and pretty much said, "Job, you wanted to come here to this earth, so I gave you a mission and a purpose to fulfill. Stand up like a man now and fulfill it!" Job broke out of his despair, refocused, and reoriented himself to his purpose here on earth.

You, too, were sent from the presence of God to this earth to fulfill a high and noble calling. Meditate on these things and let these biblical truths fill you with awe. This world is not your home. You are here on a mission. Not all of the children of God have or will come to this earth. However, you were chosen. Not everyone fulfills his or her mission or purpose for being here either. Through the Cross of Jesus, you entered into the Kingdom of God. Your mission is to bring Heaven to earth. It is God's purpose that you someday will return home a much greater, nobler spirit in the image and likeness of Jesus Christ.

Your spirit is very old and knows much more than what your mind has comprehended so far. When your heart and mind agree, all things are possible to you in Christ Jesus. Ask. Knock. Seek. Search for the truth and let it set you free.

The Spirit of Man

Your spirit is the real you. God is breaking the outer person so that you can live from your spirit and not your soul. Many Christians' spirits are encased within the soul, trapped by the physical body, and beat down by appetites of the flesh. God is cracking the outer core so the Spirit will beam forth from our spirit.

God put His own genetic code in your spirit. His "seed" abides in you, encased in your spirit. You are born not of a corruptible seed, but an incorruptible seed by the Word of God, which lives and abides inside of you. Every Spirit-filled believer is born of incorruptible seed:

> *No one who is born of God practices sin, because His seed abides in him; and he cannot sin, because he is born of God* (1 John 3:9).

The Greek word for "seed" is *sperma*. We have the divine *sperma* of God in our spirit. God's entire DNA is inside of us.

In the natural, all of the DNA of the father is in the seed, and it says a lot about how someone will turn out, like hair and eye color and even personality type. Our genetic makeup is "programmed" in the father's seed.

You were born again of the seed of God. All of God's DNA is residing within you. The spiritual genetic DNA of God was placed into you, and in it are all of the characteristics of the Lord. Now if all of that seed that is in you reaches maturity, who do you think you will be like? Jesus! That seed is inside of you. You do not have to struggle to get those characteristics—they are all within you, already there. However, even though God put His very own nature into our spirit, most of us live out of the soul. This is important to lay hold of—it is already placed within you, but everything emerges through faith. Faith, though, comes by understanding, and understanding is vital to the maturation process.

The Seed of God

Maturation happens when Christ grows to maturity from the seed God planted in your spirit until you are fully formed in the image and the likeness of Him. Your personality does not change, but your spirit becomes a perfect "clone" of the Lord Jesus Christ living in and through you. You do not have to fast and seek God for these characteristics or for His nature—all of it is already in you by reason of the new birth.

In the natural, people reach adulthood between 18 and 23 years of age and then develop into maturity. However, as far as spiritual growth is concerned, some people simply don't grow or mature at all while others mature instantly or within a few years. God is after growth in your spirit, and the process involves a breaking of the outward person. In this breaking process, God may use pressures, troubles, circumstances, or disappointments along with revelation of His Word to break the soul encasement. That is the outer shell that we come to depend on or rely on. For an analogy, maturation is a process not unlike the metamorphosis of a caterpillar to a butterfly. The cocoon is a protective encasement from which the butterfly must eventually emerge; otherwise the cocoon becomes a prison, and the living thing within ultimately dies because it has not broken through.

The Galatians, who comprised part of the early Church, experienced stunted growth because they reverted to the Law, which stopped movement in the spirit. Paul told them, in essence, that they had started the journey in the spirit but finished the whole thing in the flesh, or soul. It is impossible to mature this way because Christ, being fully formed in us, comes by the spirit not reverting to the soul. I believe that one of God's near plans will be to sweep across the Body of Christ with a baptism of fire to renovate the soul of humankind so the Spirit can beam forth.

The Church today has been in this place of stunted growth for too long. Do we feel as though we have to discipline ourselves first to get to that place of being holy before we become acceptable to God so that He can use us? That is called "works," and that is not how things are supposed to happen. When you are born again, all of God's nature was placed into your spirit. You have the package; I have the package; every Spirit-filled believer has the package! All we have to do is release and acknowledge Christ in us because His DNA and characteristics in us cannot sin or fail. His DNA in us is pure, faultless, sinless, and unfailing. Thus, the one born of God does not sin.

Try preaching that to a church! Nevertheless, it is true. We must have revelation of that which is perfect—the DNA of God that He placed in our spirits, the DNA that cannot sin. Yes, you can sin with your soul, but that holy DNA in your spirit—the DNA born of God—cannot sin.

This is why there is a battle between the soul and spirit. Ultimately, God wants the inner person to emerge victorious.

Complete in Him

And in Him you have been made complete, and He is the head over all rule and authority (Colossians 2:10).

You are complete in Him—you do not need any more than that. Some of us are of the mindset that if we pray, somehow God will give us more. That is not the case because God has already given us everything we need. There is no more. All the treasures of wisdom and knowledge are in Him, and all of Him is in that divine seed which has been planted in each of us (see Col. 2:3). This is why the apostle Paul said that we have the mind of Christ.

> *For who has known the mind of the Lord, that he will instruct Him? But we have the mind of Christ* (1 Corinthians 2:16).

It is not about having more of the mind of Christ, but tapping into the fullness of what is already programmed in there—all wisdom and knowledge. All of who God is resides in your spirit. He can't give you any more than all. You are complete in Him. In Him dwells the fullness of the Godhead—this is also in you. When you get this, when the Body of Christ gets this truth and lays hold of it, the Church as we know it will be transformed into a mature Bride. God wants to bring forth sons and daughters of God in the earth. This is what He is after in these endtimes—a people who have the fullness and completeness of God flowing from them.

> *You are from God, little children, and have overcome them; because greater is He who is in you than he who is in the world* (1 John 4:4).

In the soul you are little, but in the spirit you are invincible in God. You have the mind of Christ—all wisdom and knowledge; you know all things.

> *But you have an anointing from the Holy One, and you know all things* (1 John 2:20 NKJV)

> *But when He, the Spirit of truth, comes, He will guide you into all the truth . . . and He will disclose to you what is to come* (John 16:13).

The real you is not an insignificant person, for you are made in the image and likeness of God. This whole world awaits a manifestation, a coming forth, a revealing of people who will walk in the image and the likeness of God. This requires putting the soul life to death and placing your will, thoughts, emotions, and desires into subjection to your spirit.

> *But as for you, the anointing (the sacred appointment, the unction) which you received from Him abides [permanently] in you; [so] then you have no need that anyone should instruct you. But just as His anointing teaches you concerning everything and is true and is no falsehood, so you must abide in (live in, never depart from) Him [being rooted in Him, knit to Him], just as [His anointing] has taught you [to do]* (1 John 2:27 AMP).

The new person is in you.

> *Therefore, if anyone is in Christ, he is a new creation; old things have passed away; behold, all things have become new* (2 Corinthians 5:17 NKJV).

You are a new creation in Christ!

You Are "gods"?

> *Jesus answered them, "Has it not been written in your Law 'I said, you are gods'?"* (John 10:34).

In Chapter 8, I briefly brought out the little "god" human factor. Jesus is quoting from Psalm 82:6 and says that we are gods (see John 10:34). What a thing to say as He was about to be stoned for saying that He is the one who gives eternal life and that He and the Father are One.

There was a time I could hardly bring myself to think of it, much less say it. Just the mere mention of it causes the traditional thinking of most Christians to say that this type of teaching is "off the wall." Let me make this clear from the outset. There is only one God. God Himself came up with a God-count. There is One, and One only, God.

> *Thus says the Lord, the King of Israel and his Redeemer, the Lord of hosts: "I am the first and I am the last, and there is no God besides Me.... Do not tremble and do not be afraid; have I not long since announced it to you and declared it? And you are My witnesses is there any God besides Me, or is there any other Rock? I know of none"* (Isaiah 44:6,8).

"You are gods" is one of the strangest statements in the Bible and one that many just gloss over because of a lack of understanding. Most of us are able to live with that lack, but the Bible does tell us to get wisdom and understanding (see Prov. 4:5-7).

This was not a question of Christ classifying people as deity but as the offspring of deity. We are the spiritual sons and daughters of God the Father, partakers of His divine nature and appointed as His representatives to rule and govern in the kingdom territory called earth. Jesus was not saying that we would be gods in our own right or added to the Godhead in any way. Our mandate is and always has been to come to be like God (see 1 John 3:2).

Jesus was quoting from Psalm 82:

> *God stands in the assembly [of the representatives] of God; in the midst of the magistrates or judges He gives judgment [as] among the gods.... I said, "You are gods [since you judge on My behalf, as My representatives]; indeed, all of you are children of the Most High"* (Psalm 82:1,6 AMP).

In both scriptural references, the Hebrew word *elohim* is used in the context of gods being magistrates and judges appointed by God as His representatives or delegates.

Christ was saying that we are all children and family of the Most High God. If we are family, then we are born of divine seed, made in God's image. Children look like their parents usually, don't they? We are gods (small "g") because we are God's children and because we act as His earthly representatives, judging and acting on His behalf. This word *elohim* is the same word used in Genesis 1 referring to God the Creator: *"In the beginning God* [Elohim] *created the heavens and the earth"* (Gen. 1:1). As His children and delegates, we are God's "creator gods" (lower-case) in the earth, establishing His earthly government as ambassadors of His supernatural Kingdom.

We need to understand that through the love of the Father and the plan of God, He reconciled humanity to fellowship with Himself, and in so doing, restored us to our rightful place as sons and daughters in the Kingdom of God. We are partakers of the divine nature and have been freed from the curse of the Law, being raised up to a heavenly state of being and seated with Jesus in authority far above all rule and dominion.

As family members—sons and daughters—we have been made joint-heirs with Jesus, and as He is, so are we in this world. The Glory the Father had given to Jesus He has given to us, along with the full right as family members to be called the children of God.

We as children of God must see ourselves in our rightful place of power and authority on earth. The truth of God's Word will bring us all of the revelation we need for transformation, to get us living as victorious conquerors in Christ.

God called his newly created, formed, and framed firstborn son "very good." When the Father breathed into Adam's nostrils, the breath of life, all of the DNA of the Creator, was deposited into him body, soul, and spirit. Adam was a supernatural being with the ability to create and co-create with God. He had a dual nature with full access to the unseen realm as well as the natural. He was God's offspring, a son of His love, fruit of His own nature, created in His image.

The word *image* means "reflection or direct projection of the object in the exact likeness." Jesus was the Image of the invisible God. He declared boldly, "He who has seen Me has seen the Father" (John 14:9).

Jesus and the Father were One. Jesus is the outshining of the Father's Glory, the projection of the invisible God, and we are made in His image. As we abide in Him and He abides in us, we have access into the heavenlies and are able to move in power and authority in the earth.

> *And He has put all things under His feet and has appointed Him the universal and supreme Head of the church [a headship exercised throughout the church], which is His body, the fullness of Him Who fills all in all [for in that body lives the full measure of Him Who makes everything complete, and Who fills everything everywhere with Himself]* (Ephesians 1:22-23 AMP).

We, the Church, are the full measure of Christ in the earth, complete in Him, bone of His bone, and flesh of His flesh. We are the image of God, and having the revelation of this alive inside of us is the beginning of complete and total victory. We must understand who we are in Him.

Only Humanity

We need to understand that all of creation is beautiful and wonderful in its own way—the plants, the trees, the angels, the planetary system—but only humans are the same species as God.

> *God said, "Let Us [Father, Son, and Holy Spirit] make mankind in Our image, after Our likeness, and let them have complete authority over the fish of the sea, the birds*

*of the air, the [tame] beasts, and over all of the earth,
and over everything that creeps upon the earth"* (Genesis
1:26 AMP).

He only created humans in His image and His likeness as His
offspring. The created angelic realm is not the same as we are. When
God created Adam it says in Genesis 2:7 that He formed man from
the dust of the ground and breathed into his nostrils the breath
or Spirit of life, and man became a living being. In Creation, only
Adam was fashioned by the hand of God, and it was only Adam who
received the life-giving Spirit breath from the mouth of God. Adam
was gathered and formed from the newly created dust of the ground
in the natural realm and was breathed into with the eternal Spirit
DNA of God to become the first man born of God—the first of the
family and same species as God!

The Creation Law of Reproduction

There is a prevailing law in creation established before the foundation of the world called "The Creation Law of Reproduction," which
simply means all things reproduce after their own kind.

> *Then God said, "Let the earth sprout vegetation, plants
> yielding seed, and fruit trees on the earth bearing fruit
> after their kind with seed in them"; and it was so. The
> earth brought forth vegetation, plants yielding seed after
> their kind...and God saw that it was good* (Genesis
> 1:11-12).

God's design was that everything created would "bring forth" after
its own kind. Think about it! Birds are birds; they bring forth birds after
their likeness. Fish are fish; they bring forth fish each after their own
kind and likeness. Cattle bring forth cattle. An apple tree brings forth

apples. God brought forth a son after His own kind, a family member that was formed, fashioned, and equipped with His DNA to look like Him and act like Him, even creating and co-creating with Him in the earth! God walked and talked with Adam in the cool of the day in relationship. Adam was completely natural and supernatural, spiritual and physical. *"Then the Lord God took the man and put him into the garden of Eden to cultivate it and keep it"* (Gen. 2:15).

The word *Eden* means *delight;* God made us to live in delight. The Garden itself was massive, hundreds if not thousands of square miles in diameter. How was it that Adam was to tend, guard, and keep the Garden? Remember Adam was just like his Father.

Adam accomplished his God-appointed tasks by supernatural ability. He was an authoritative son of Glory moving without restraint in the earth. By subduing knowledge, wisdom, and understanding, all Adam had to do was think of what needed to be accomplished, and as he spoke it was created. All he needed to do was simply speak of the place he needed to be and he was there and the task was completed just as he imagined it. Adam moved back and forth on the earth in the spiritual dimension, as quick as a thought, just as the angels of God did.

Adam acted as a literal son of the Most High God. He was fully engaged in spirit, soul, and body at all times and his connection or fellowship with Heaven was never broken.

[CHAPTER 12]

THE POWER OF THE TRANSFORMED MIND

Satan is very much aware of the power of the transformed mind and constantly assaults our minds, which are his greatest battlefields. Whoever wins the battle for our minds is whose servants we'll become. Paul commanded us to think on virtuous things. We cannot allow our minds to dwell upon evil or things that are incompatible with God and expect to be compatible with Him.

> *Do not be deceived: "Evil company corrupts good habits"*
> (1 Corinthians 15:33 NKJV).

We have within us the ability to renew our minds and be transformed. The mind is malleable. Humankind has a creative capacity. We operate in that capacity either consciously or unconsciously. Thoughts are seeds. When thoughts are connected with strong emotion, they become seeds and conception takes place. If that seed is nurtured and incubated, it will reproduce according to the particular framework of that particular pattern of thought, whether for evil or for good. Seed thoughts will manifest and come to pass! One of the most important laws of the Kingdom is that all things reproduce after their own likeness and kind. Your thoughts will reproduce after their own kind.

The Programmable Mind

The minds of people are difficult to understand. The human brain is an incredible bioelectric, magnetic mass of gray matter and works similar to a computer. We use our brains to think, to analyze and disseminate information, and to arrive at conclusions. Although a computer cannot originate thought, it is programmable. The mind is programmable too. It can be programmed with ideas, concepts, knowledge, and values and will run according to its programming. Satan wants to program your mind to run according to his program with lies and values that are contrary to God's thoughts and ways.

Just watch some television for a while and see how many anti-God concepts vie for mind space. There's a very real all-out assault for your mind out there. The greatest battlefield in the three-fold nature of man (body, soul, and spirit) is the mind, not the spirit. Satan knows that if he can capture your mind your thinking will be out of kilter and then the whole person will be off.

When your mind is single, your eye will be single, and your whole body will be full of light. When your mind is free and clean, the doorway is open for God's love and light to flow in and through you. We all need to get our thought lives aligned with the purposes of God and His Word and understand the way that He thinks.

The good news is that God sent us an instruction manual that explains the marvel of the mind and how to use it. That book is the Bible, and it reveals valuable keys to the right and proper use of the mind. It explains why we're incapable, in and of ourselves, of working out His purpose without His divine intervention.

A Receptor and Gateway

When thoughts and emotions blend, a creative process of birthing starts in the thought life and in the realm of the imagination. Satan knows this, so the battle is for who controls your mind. The mind is a receptor and open to spiritual influences, both light and dark. Jesus talks about dark light in Matthew 6:23. Dark light is the belief that something is true when in actuality it is not. This is deception. The inference is to be careful of the thing you believe to be light, when indeed it is dark. Why? Because the mind is the gateway and connector to all incoming spiritual communication.

The mind is a part of the physical body. The brain is a physical organ and an incredible bioelectronic computer capable of processing thought. The physical brain is different from the mind. The brain is the physical housing and connector used by the mind to translate spiritually inspired information communicated from the realm of the spirit. The brain then transfers this information into the natural. Bill Johnson states that "God didn't design the mind to be an originator of thought." Rather, He designed the mind to act as an internal processor capable of receiving programmable information—information that could be programmed into the "system."[1]

Whoever programs your mind will determine the way you think and how your life evolves—what your life will become, or your destiny. For within your mind is the foundation of what you really believe about what you believe and the associated emotions that stem from and reinforce the choices you make. Satan will try to win the right to your mind so that he can program it just the way he wants.

However, God created the human spirit with the ability to receive inspired supernatural information directly from Him and with the capacity to direct and influence the mind, will, emotions, and flesh to manifest in the natural what we receive from Him in the spirit. Consider that God is Spirit, and He created humankind with the very breath of His Spirit. Humans, as spirit, have the capacity to create and originate thought. This is the wonderful and powerful dimension from which all miracles, signs, and wonders come that manifest from the realm of Glory.

Human Intellect

On earth, humans are the only created beings that possess a spirit, intellect, and reason. We also have thoughts, emotions, and behaviors unique to us as spirit beings created in the image of God.

Humans are capable of loving God; the inferior creatures are not. This is the specific difference between people and animals. The animal kingdom relies on instinct—inborn behaviors that are still baffling to science. How does a salmon know to swim to where it was born to lay its eggs and die? How do birds know how far to fly south? How do homing pigeons know to find their way home?

We can originate thought, but animals cannot. Everything animals know has been preprogrammed or may be programmed into them. We, on the other hand, don't instinctively know everything we need to know. The psalmist wrote, *"...I am fearfully and wonderfully made..."* (Ps. 139:14). This is true of your brain. It is amazing, but it is also incomplete in that we must constantly acquire physical and spiritual knowledge.

Acquiring Knowledge

We gain physical knowledge with our five senses. We see, hear, smell, touch, and taste and constantly add to our knowledge base. We gain spiritual knowledge in a similar way by developing and using our spiritual senses. When we draw close to God and allow God to strengthen, teach, and lead us through and by His Spirit, spiritual desires spring forth and we accomplish spiritual things. With a Spirit-led mind, we will find the way into that supernatural realm of God's Kingdom and all of its treasures. If we can spiritually see God's Kingdom, how much more will we desire it?

The spirit of humankind was designed by God to receive knowledge and understanding. We call this revelation. With it we decipher information from the physical world with our five senses, and we can see, touch, smell, hear, and taste things from the spiritual realm by God's Spirit.

Each of us has the privilege and awesome responsibility of programming our own brain, and we will "run" according to this programming. The Bible says, *"Train up a child in the way he should go, even when he is old he will not depart from it"* (Prov. 22:6). What we program into the life of a child may govern his or her life in adulthood. What we program into our minds will govern our lives.

If we program our children right when they are young, they won't depart from it when they are old. A child may deviate from the program from time to time, but eventually he or she will "run" according to the programming.

Sometimes we end up with wrong programming that runs contrary to the design of God; however, when we are born again, we are supernaturally infused with the holy seed of God. In that very seed is *all* of who God is. In time, with the proper care from the Holy Spirit and the Word, that seed will grow and bear the exact likeness and makeup of the original Seed. Contained in the seed is all of who God is spiritually and the very likeness and image of Christ Jesus.

When Mind and Spirit Agree

...and that from childhood you have known the sacred writings which are able to give you the wisdom that leads to salvation through faith which is in Christ Jesus (2 Timothy 3:15).

When you examine an acorn, it seems impossible that a huge tree is in that seed, but it is. Given the right climate and soil conditions, it will naturally become a huge tree. So too, with the Seed of God planted in you, given the right conditions, you'll grow to become like Him. Planted in you is the very mind of Christ. Deep within your spirit—which is joined to the Holy Spirit—is the mind of Christ Jesus. He who is joined to the Lord is one spirit:

> *Only conduct yourselves in a manner worthy of the gospel of Christ, so that whether I come and see you or remain absent, I will hear of you that you are standing firm in one sprit, with one mind striving together for the faith of the gospel* (Philippians 1:27).

Reprogramming Your Mind

Light will flow into your being and the transformation process will begin when there's harmony between your mind and your spirit. Harmony comes through freedom from blockages, renewal, and reprogramming of the mind.

If your mind runs against the truth, the Seed in your spirit cannot grow. Cast out everything that is not the truth of God's Word, and the truth will renew your mind and you'll see rapid growth in your life. Quickened truth is when revelation comes and you receive it. Revelation carries with it the power to renew your mind.

> *For who has known or understood the mind (the counsels and purposes) of the Lord so as to guide and instruct Him and give Him knowledge?* (1 Corinthians 2:16 AMP)

Your mind is the gateway between the spirit and physical realm for the whole person, so your mind and spirit must agree. When you were born again your spirit and mind were no longer compatible, so it's an ongoing process to reprogram the mind to conform to the mind of Christ in your spirit.

Deposited in your spirit person is the mind of Christ. Yes, your spirit has a mind—the mind of Christ! Consider Ephesians 4:23: *"...and that you be renewed in the spirit of your mind."*

Your mind can originate thought as part of the creative process. However, it can also be *inspired* by your spirit and the Holy Spirit within you; for example, when you instantly get a *spark of revelation* or a *knowing* of something you hadn't known previously. This will occur more and more frequently as your mind is renewed and becomes submissive to your spirit. They must be in harmony or there will be blockages. The brain will sift and sort information it receives, but unless that harmony exists with the spirit, the unrenewed mind (non-spiritual man) will toss out supernatural revelation or block it altogether.

> *But the natural, non-spiritual man does not accept or welcome or admit into his heart the gifts and teachings and revelations of the Spirit of God, for they are folly (meaningless nonsense) to him; and he is incapable of knowing them [of progressively recognizing, understanding, and becoming better acquainted with them] because they are spiritually discerned and estimated and appreciated* (1 Corinthians 2:14 AMP).

The natural mind is the mind or the soul life programmed with the concepts of this world and the kingdom of darkness. The spiritual person must be programmed with different thinking.

> *Now we have not received the spirit [that belongs to] the world, but the [Holy] Spirit Who is from God, [given to us] that we might realize and comprehend and appreciate the gifts [of divine favor and blessing so freely and lavishly] bestowed on us by God* (1 Corinthians 2:12 AMP).

But the one who joins himself to the Lord is one sprit with Him (1 Corinthians 6:17).

The First Step to Renewal

Your spirit has become one with the Lord. Everything that God is already lives in your spirit person. We are joined to the Lord and are "one spirit with Him." We must align the brain with the spirit—bringing the brain and spirit into unity so that they are not running on separate programs.

> *Do not be conformed to this world (this age), [fashioned after and adapted to its external, superficial customs], but be transformed (changed) by the [entire] renewal of your mind [by its new ideals and its new attitude], so that you may prove [for yourselves] what is the good and acceptable and perfect will of God, even the thing which is good and acceptable and perfect [in His sight for you]* (Romans 12:2 AMP).

Your brain has to be transformed from the soulish concepts of the world by the Word of God, which you receive whether you understand it or not. There are many things in the Word of God that we have yet to understand. We read things and pass them by because there is a layer there that is not coming through to us. However, God's Word is truth whether we understand it or not. And it starts with this—we accept God's Word whether we understand it or not. It is God's Word. This is the first step in renewal. The greatest hindrance to walking with God is the unrenewed brain.

> *For the rest, brethren, whatever is true, whatever is worthy of reverence and is honorable and seemly, whatever is just, whatever is pure, whatever is lovely and lovable, whatever is kind and winsome and gracious, if there is any virtue*

and excellence, if there is anything worthy of praise, think on
and weigh and take account of these things [fix your minds on
them] (Philippians 4:8 AMP).

This Scripture should guard our minds at all times. It should act as a filter that we place over our mind. If it is not true, honest, or pure, reject it. God has placed this in the Bible to keep our minds clean and running right and flowing with the light and love of God.

The apostle Paul in his letter to the Romans records an amazing statement. He said:

[That is] because the mind of the flesh [with its carnal thoughts
and purposes] is hostile to God, for it does not submit itself to
God's Law; indeed it cannot (Romans 8:7 AMP).

In other words, the natural mind is an enemy of God. This statement provides startling insight into the workings of the carnal, natural mind. Cut off from God, the mind is an enemy of God—the mind hates Him. Your spirit may be born again, but if your mind is unrenewed there is conflict. Your spirit flows through the mind and truth is blocked or corrupted and altered because of wrong concepts.

If we can get our thinking patterns renewed to be compatible with our spirit man, there will be a unity that will open a supernatural gateway from Heaven that will allow light, understanding, and knowledge to flow into our being and transform us. It is then that we will understand the mysteries of creation and the universe. We will understand God and the purposes of God because our brains will be in harmony with Him. The supernatural pathways only open when the two become compatible.

An Ancient Spirit

As mentioned in Chapter 11, your spirit came from Heaven and has been in existence for a long time. I am talking spirit here, not the soul.

The soul can die. God can take the soul, or the soul can be forfeited by a person. The soul can also be saved and redeemed (see Ps. 86:13; 116:4; 2 Sam. 4:9). Therefore, the soul is what each person is as a human being. A person cannot exist outside of the soul. The Old Testament reveals nothing about any preexistence or immortality of the soul.

But the spirit is another matter. It pre-existed in Heaven; however, it is clothed in the soul. Your spirit came into your body at birth. It was God's intention that we grow beyond just spirit and become a new creation. That's why Paul prays:

> ...and may your spirit and soul and body be preserved sound and complete [and found] blameless at the coming of our Lord Jesus Christ (the Messiah) (1 Thessalonians 5:23 AMP).

It is important that we as spirit, soul, and body blend as one so we can interact with the spiritual realm and the physical realm. Heaven was first a spiritual world. But God created the earth and brought Heaven to earth, bringing it into a physical dimension. When you were born again Christ came into your spirit. That seed is more than just spirit. You are a living soul and the mind is the key.

In a previous chapter, we talked about living and moving by the Law of the Spirit. The Book of Romans tells us that to be spiritually minded is life and peace, but to be carnally minded is death. The natural mind has programming from another kingdom, the kingdom of darkness. When your spirit longs and yearns to move in the light, your brain objects and unbelief often stops you in your tracks because your brain runs counter to what is in your spirit. If we can get the brain and spirit in harmony, we will do incredible things.

What you feed your brain is of utmost importance. The battle is on for programming rights to your brain. Whoever gets it gets you. Yes, the Holy Spirit can and does erase wrong programming; however, keeping it programmed is vital. If you do not keep your mind programmed right, you will fall back into the mess you came out of.

Demons or evil spirits can lodge over the brain to control or influence the pathways of thinking and corrupt the imagination. They filter any pure light of revelation coming to us. When this happens, a person needs deliverance. The demonic spirit realm can and does influence us, and if we allow it entry it may attach itself to our thought life or our imagination, creating a spiritual stronghold.

Evil spirits build strongholds, and they attach themselves to us as a false concept or way of thinking. They clothe our minds, projecting unclean thoughts into our thinking, strengthening untruths. If we refuse them the doors or pathways will close. The more we close the doors, the better; they will eventually give up. We have to be diligent door-closers because the spirits have an incredible capacity to interact with the brain as they project pictures, thoughts, or concepts. If we do not object—if we do not slam the door shut—they may nest in our minds and even multiply.

Start Now

Our dreams and vision must be in line with what God has called us to and what our future is. If we can start to get even a small amount of compatibility between our spirit and our brain, we will start to fill up with light. We will see the wonders of God. We will begin to understand like never before. The creative side of our life will begin to blossom, and we will begin to flow into our destiny.

Many people have a destiny and never fulfill it because they can't see it and don't believe it. Their minds are not big enough to accommodate their destiny. The spirit is certainly big enough, but the brain is limited.

Listen—getting started is a good thing. God will have a supernatural people, a Glory generation in these last days that will do great things that we have never thought possible. We have to be changed now—we have to become the overcoming Body of Christ—if we with Christ will rule the world. We have to align our mind and spirit if we're to do the "all things are possible." We can have such an impact on the Glory harvest when we enlarge our thinking by aligning it with our spirit. Going to church every Sunday will not do it, but having Heaven's mind will.

Take Back Your Mind

The battlefield is in the mind. We have a fierce adversary who wants control of it. How do we take it back? By the casting down of imaginations and of every high thing that exalts itself against the knowledge of God. Thus, we are to bring every thought into captivity and into the obedience of Christ (see 2 Cor. 10:5).

Our lives have to become so transparent that people see Jesus through our life experiences and actions. During the time of transition into the Millennial Kingdom, Jesus will take an active place as the Head of His "corporate Body." This will give expression to His life and ministry in the same way that He functioned through a single body during His time on earth. All that Jesus did in a single body He will do again through the corporate Body as an end-time witness to the nations, giving some to be apostles, some prophets, some evangelists, and some pastors and teachers for the work of the ministry.

Through an act of intervention, we are about to be lifted into the spirit realm, where ministry will function through relationship rather than through gifting. There we'll find straight paths to the hidden riches of secret places.

> *Thus says the Lord to His anointed, to Cyrus, whose right hand I have held—to subdue nations before him and loose the armor of kings, to open before him the double doors, so that the gates will not be shut: "I will go before you and make the crooked places straight; I will break in pieces the gates of bronze and cut the bars of iron. I will give you the treasures of darkness and hidden riches of secret places, that you may know that I, the Lord, who call you by your*

name, am the God of Israel (Isaiah 45:1-3 NKJV).

Jesus knew all about straight paths. He could and did walk through walls. As we mature in sonship, renewing our minds for transformation, we too will have the ability to seamlessly walk in the seemingly impossible. We can breach walls of resistance and walls built to keep us out. When we come through them to the other side, we won't know how we got there, just as Peter didn't understand how he was able to walk on water, because walking in the ways of the law of the Spirit defies all natural reasoning. To those walking with the wind of the Spirit, to those walking in the power of a transformed mind, to those walking in compatibility with God as co-heirs, God says the gates shall not be shut.

These spiritual gates open wide to the spiritual sons and daughters of God who will find access into Eden's door and to the Tree of Life. They are destiny's double doors that will open for you to encounter God in genuine, tangible ways, executing and partaking of the ever-increasing and all-powerful realm of Glory in the Kingdom of God for His Glory. Are you ready to break into new dimensions of the realities of the Glory realm of God?

Endnote

1. Bill Johnson, *The Supernatural Power of the Renewed Mind,* audio teaching (Redding, CA: Bethel Church).

CHAPTER 13

THE CREATIVE POWER
OF THOUGHTS

In this chapter, we will touch on several subjects I introduced in Chapter 12, "The Power of the Transformed Mind." These review topics will serve as a platform to launch us into deeper understanding and teaching on the mind, specifically the creative power of thoughts. As this lesson unfolds, you'll understand more of the inner workings and intricate mechanics of the mind and thought life.

Metamorphosis

The Greek word *metamorphoo* is translated into the English word *transformed* as found in Romans 12. The word *metamorphoo* actually means *metamorphosis,* which is the process a caterpillar goes through in the cocoon—it enters as a larva and leaves as a beautiful butterfly.

And do not be conformed to this world, but be transformed
by the renewing of your mind, so that you may prove what

the will of God is, that which is good and acceptable and perfect (Romans 12:2).

A caterpillar crawls along the ground and conforms to all of the earth's contours. A butterfly, on the other hand, soars above the earth. Paul is exhorting the believers in Rome not to conform to the world with its traditions and ways of thinking. He is saying that our entire lives will be transformed and metamorphosed when our minds are renewed. This will allow us to soar and not have to conform to the world's standards of living and being; we'll be fully capable of proving the good and acceptable and perfect will of God.

A *mindset* is when our minds are programmed and set to respond a specific way or project a certain impression when encountering different words, pictures, situations, et cetera. For example, when the word *church* is stated, many have a very definite impression about the topic. They have preconceived thoughts and feelings about church because of previous experiences that have been grafted into their minds: a church they attended when they were younger, a religious fanatic they watched on television, or the enthusiastic preacher on the car radio.

For most of us, our mindsets are in the caterpillar state—the worm that is still conformed to this world. That mindset, however, is about to be changed and renewed. The Bride of Christ is about to become a very heavenly creature. Many people will look for her crawling along the ground but will miss her as she soars overhead.

Ungodly and worldly mindsets are spiritual strongholds that restrain us from soaring. These bondages are broken by the transformation that comes from the pressure and isolation in the cocoon. The Greek word *thlipsis* is translated into the English word *tribulation,* which literally means *pressure.* We are liberated through the constrictions and pressures that the Lord allows to come upon us in the cocoon. The restraints of self-dependence are broken as we rely more and more on the Spirit of God, being strengthened in our inner person so we can rise to higher altitudes. Those who want to avoid these trials will be confined as worms to the earth.

We can choose to move with the current of the Spirit and let the trials of this present age work for us, or we can continue to wade through the shallow water and never reach our destination, which only comes after the rapids. Jesus said, *"Whoever finds his [lower] life will lose it [the higher life], and whoever loses his [lower] life on My account will find it [the higher life]"* (Matt. 10:39 AMP). Paul said the sufferings and tribulations of this present age are not even worthy to be compared to the Glory that will be revealed to us, in us, and through us (see Rom. 8:18)

Unfortunately, many leaders, from a lack of maturity, have restrained and kept the Church in a state of infancy; they are in danger of loosing all. This metamorphosis is mandatory. Trying to save someone from it is doing him harm. The chick needs the struggle of getting out of the egg to produce blood flow into its extremities. If not, there's a good chance of loosing its life after birth. The struggle for life is necessary for walking in the fullness of life.

The Most Excellent Way

Humans, like God, have a creative ability that can be exercised through the mind to recreate the world around us. Psalm 139:14 says that we are "fearfully and wonderfully made." We were created in the image and likeness of God. The same creative nature of God is resident within humankind. Creative authority is best released through love—the most excellent way.

With all that has been given to humanity in terms of the gifts of the Holy Spirit and the ability to cooperate with the Spirit of God in the anointing, there still remains a fuller and more abundant way to minister the mind, heart, and power of God in the earth.

Paul says, *"But earnestly desire and zealously cultivate the greatest and best gifts and graces (the higher gifts and the choicest graces). And yet I will show you a still more excellent way..."* (1 Cor. 12:31 AMP). What is the more excellent way? Love!

For we know in part and we prophesy in part; but when the perfect comes, the partial will be done away. When I was a child, I used to speak like a child, think like a child, reason like a child; when I became a man, I did away with childish things. For now we see in a mirror dimly, but then face to face; now I know in part, but then I will know fully just as I also have been fully known. But now faith, hope, love, abide these three; but the greatest of these is love (1 Corinthians 13:9-13).

Many people take the phrase, "when the perfect comes," and conclude it is referring to the second coming of Christ. The phrase, however, is talking about love. The whole chapter is talking about love and our lives being perfected in love. Paul is talking about a new standard, a new level. He says we should earnestly desire the best gifts and graces, but there still is a better way—the way of love. What are the childish things Paul is referring to? They are "in part" and "partial." The childish things that we are called to put away are *knowing in part* and *understanding in part,* so we can *entirely* and *fully* know Him who is Love.

This Glory move of God will be carried out with the stamp of Galatians 5:6: *"...faith working through love."* Without this quality of love, we will never be connected with the heart of God in this most excellent way. When that which is perfect is come, looking through a glass darkly will be done away with. We will come to this perfection of love—from one level to another—more fully, deeply, and intimately.

Thoughts Birthed from Passion

It is important for us to keep in mind that thoughts are seeds. Thoughts have life in them and will reproduce. As we talked about earlier, the "Creation Law of Reproduction" simply means all things reproduce after their own kind. Genesis 1:11-12 says the earth brought forth grass and herbs yielding seed after their kind and trees yielding fruit that produced seed after its own kind.

This creation law affects us continually as it shapes our future and determines our present. Even now our circumstances are being determined by this law. We need to stop blaming everybody and their brother, including the devil, for our present circumstances and to take responsibility for what is growing in our lives.

This creation law is irrevocable and unchangeable. We plant trees and gardens, and they reproduce after their kind. The fertile soil where we unknowingly plant most seeds is in the garden of our heart. What you plant there will reproduce and come forth. Thoughts are simply seeds. Passion and strong desire are the heat that causes the seed to spin into life. Babies are conceived in passion. So too, inner passion gives life to the seeds in our heart.

For as he thinks in his heart, so is he (Proverbs 23:7 NKJV).

This means that as a person believes and thinks in his heart, so he will become. What he thinks about will be manifested in his life. In Matthew 7:1-2, Jesus says that if you judge, you will be judged; and in the same measure you judge with, you will be judged also. The seed of judgment sown will reap a tree of judgment. Because of this law, we must live every moment, in thought and action, as we desire the future to be.

The human mind is one of the greatest earthly powers. This is why Jesus said

> *Truly I say to you, whoever says to this mountain, "Be taken up and cast into the sea," and does not doubt in his heart, but believes that what he says is going to happen, it will be granted him* (Mark 11:23).

Jesus isn't speaking metaphorically—He's talking literally. You don't even have to be a Christian for this to work. There are many people displaying supernatural feats and abilities illegally by this principle alone.

Remember, the human mind is a great earthly power; this universal law cannot be changed.

Jesus goes on to further explain this truth: *"For this reason I am telling you, whatever you ask for in prayer, believe (trust and be confident) that it is granted to you, and you will [get it]"* (Mark 11:24 AMP).

Jesus is saying to believe, be confident, and desire what you are asking for and you will receive it. Our thoughts aren't momentary insignificant wisps but are the seeds of desire that produce and chart the course of our present and future life. If thoughts are seeds, then how are they planted?

When a thought firmly connects with emotion, a supernatural power or force is released. If you hold your thoughts until they are connected with your emotions, feelings, and desires, it releases the power of life and light. This principle is similar to *"...if two of you agree on earth about anything...it shall be done for them..."* (Matt. 18:19).

When your emotions agree with your thinking, it shall be done! This is the power of union and agreement. It works for both God-thoughts and demonic thoughts. For example: love. Your husband or wife comes home from work and gives you a big kiss and tells you with warm affection you are loved. When the connection takes place between your thoughts and your emotions, it begins to fill your entire being and becomes a living force. This seed of thought, when energized by emotion, will literally create an environment of love and joy around your entire household.

Any thoughts that connect with our emotions become a very strong power and determine the atmosphere around us. The Church has taught for years that emotions are not important. I say to you that emotions as well as your thought life are the creative side of you. Your emotions are essential for everything to happen. Jesus was moved with an emotion called compassion and released miracles (see Matt. 20:34; Mark 1:41). Compassion releases miracles, even the raising of the dead (see Luke 7:11-17).

The power and Glory of God in the anointing are released through the gateway of human affection. This is why Paul says, *"...you are restricted by your own affections"* (2 Cor. 6:12 NKJV). We have to feel what we do. When our thinking connects with our feelings, a seed is planted by desire and a power is released. James says, *"Then, when desire has conceived, it gives birth to sin; and sin, when it is full-grown, brings forth death"* (James 1:15 NKJV).

We need to be careful what we are thinking! Every time we think, we place a spiritual offering at the door that energizes and powers that thought. An evil desire is *conceived* when the thought and the emotion come together. This forms a creative power bond of agreement that *brings forth* death. *Brings forth* means to breed or create and is the same as a plant that is produced from the seed. It is the "Creation Law of Reproduction" at work.

When I meditate on the Word and revelation begins to flow, my whole being seems to be flooded with light—not only light, but flooded with the tranquil peace and life of God. The revelation that is coming from God's mind flows through my emotions and makes a place in my spirit man for seed to be planted and to grow.

Revelation isn't just an abstract thought; it is connected with a feeling that buries life deep inside us. Seeds are planted; conception has taken place. If watered, the revelation with give birth in our life. As a man thinks, so he will become.

Taking Back the Imagination

As I briefly mentioned earlier, there are keys we need to employ to unlock the realm of Glory, such as vision, imagination, and faith. This new Glory generation will move in the understanding of how to release wonders in the creative power of the imagination. They will birth the will and purposes of God in the earth with mind-blowing authority over physical elements in the natural realm.

The creative power of the imagination is not a New Age or occult principle; it is a Kingdom reality created by God to manifest in the natural what is seen in the spirit. The demonic world of the occult can use it to birth destruction in the natural by curses that materialize from unholy allegiances. But God really gave us an imagination to come under the influence of the Holy Spirit and birth life, freedom, and destiny into our lives. Unfortunately, we've been taught to believe that anything to do with using our imagination is New Age and is used to advance the kingdom of darkness. In reality, New Agers and the occult stole something very precious from the saints of God and have perverted it to the point that we are afraid to come near it. It is time we take the power to envision back. It is time we start using what God has given to us to wreak havoc on the kingdom of darkness!

We must visualize what we desire to become in God. Actually, we must see ourselves as we really are in Christ; then it will manifest as reality in our lives. The imagination is a creative tool that brings into the physical world that which sits dormant in the unseen realm. We can use our imagination to transform the world around us, both for good and for evil.

You cannot walk in something until you see yourself walking in it. You say, "Visualizing is New Age." You've been visualizing since you were born. Every time you think about something, every time you daydream, you're visualizing. It's part of the thinking process. There have been a number of people throughout history who have broken through simple spiritual concepts into the upper Kingdom realities. They understood genuine Kingdom laws and began to practice them. Only a handful of people have risen to a level in God where they could overcome any earthly obstacle in life—even overcoming death. Not just Enoch either.

It is easy to blame the devil and others for things that happen to us in life, but in actuality our present circumstances are the direct result of where our heart is set in thought. We are reaping the harvest of what we have thought, envisioned, and sown.

Jesus considered the imagination as reality. He said, *"...everyone who looks at a woman with lust for her has already committed adultery with her in his heart"* (Matt. 5:28). Everyone who looks with his eyes and thinks in his mind has *committed and birthed* the act of adultery in his heart—it's already done. The mind and the imagination are the same thing. It's just as if you had already done it.

Creation Responds to Love

In every atom there is life and light. When God created the universe, He breathed them out of His imagination. The newly created atoms were all spinning harmoniously according to their own vibration, their own unique created order. However, when Adam fell from the Glory of God, the result was so dramatic that it shifted the world on its axis. The earth wasn't the only thing that shifted; each individual atom was knocked off rhythm from its original spin. Everything was affected; even at a subatomic level. When this happened, the door was wide open for satan to corrupt and alter things genetically.

The good news is that all of creation was preprogrammed to respond to love. If we have love emanating out from us, the smallest atom can feel it and will respond to it. Atoms were birthed from love, and as created particles they feel love and respond to it. Animals feel it, trees feel it, and all of nature feels it. Atoms will cooperate with what you desire and speak because they recognize your sonship and know that you have dominion over the world.

What you emanate leaves a trail and affects everything around you. If you come home with a bad attitude, before you even open your mouth, the first thing that's going to recognize it is your cat or dog. Creation knows because it is sensitized to emotion. All of creation waits eagerly for the children of God to step into their full understanding of sonship. Creation knows that we have the power and authority to free it from the bondage of decay, corruption, sin, and death that entered the world during the Fall.

> For [even the whole] creation (all nature) waits expectantly
> and longs earnestly for God's sons to be made known [waits
> for the revealing, the disclosing of their sonship.] ... That

nature (creation) itself will be set free from its bondage to decay and corruption [and gain an entrance] into the glorious freedom of God's children (Romans 8:19,21 AMP).

Remember how Paul said there was a more excellent way? When the complete and perfect comes (love), the incomplete and imperfect will vanish away (see 1 Cor. 13:10). All creation responds to the more excellent and perfect way of love. It is through love that the curse will be lifted and creation will enter into freedom. Signs, wonders, and miracles come through love—we just have to keep unbelief out.

Spirit of Unbelief

Jesus said, *"All things are possible to him who believes"* (Mark 9:23). I think it would be safe to say that not much is possible, then, if you don't believe. James says that when we ask God for something we should do it with faith and not doubt in our hearts (see James 1:6). He continues to explain what we should expect to receive from the Lord if we do indeed harbor doubt in our hearts:

> *For that man ought not to expect that he will receive anything from the Lord, being a double-minded man, unstable in all his ways* (James 1:7-8).

Doubt opens the door to unbelief, and unbelief is a tremendous evil power that cuts us off from the promises of God. Unbelief is a spirit that is like a dark, demonic hood of blindness and deception. We must deal violently with this spirit. We shouldn't have even a speck of doubt in our hearts. Jesus said, *"The time is fulfilled, and the Kingdom of God is at hand; repent and believe in the gospel"* (Mark 1:15).

Do you see that? We overcome doubt and unbelief by repenting and turning to the Lord—changing our way of thinking—then believing. Sometimes this takes a fierce step of faith in the right direction and a forceful decision to believe. It is necessary to learn to hold our focus on the Lord—to set our thoughts and our imagination in faith until they connect with our feelings and emotions. When we continually do this, heavenly seeds are planted and faith begins to grow and flourish and come alive. We must begin to see ourselves walking in the light of these things. Start to imagine yourself walking in your future and destiny, and align yourself with the Kingdom of God. It will come to pass. This is the way it is. God did it this way in the beginning: He thought it, saw it, and spoke it—then it came into existence. Remember: *"For as he thinks in his heart, so is he"* (Prov. 23:7 NKJV).

We can either believe and receive or doubt and go without. Smith Wigglesworth said, "God wants us so badly that He has made the condition as simple as He possibly could— 'Only believe.'"[1]

Unity of Spirit, Soul, and Body

There are many things that fascinate me in God, but none have come so close to the mystery of our identity in Christ. Just thinking that we have been cut out of the same swatch of clothing as God causes me to rush with anticipation. When I think about being alive in eternity before I was born or before the worlds were created, it makes me want to know the reality of that life in eternity. I want to know what it's like and what's happening there.

The reality is you are a spirit. Your spirit came from Heaven and has been in existence for a long time. Your spirit has memories of life in Heaven. However, when your spirit came into your body at birth, it became wrapped in the soul and those memories began to fade and were eventually lost.

Before Jesus was born on earth, He was a Spirit. He existed in the bosom of the Father (see John 1:18). He came to earth as a Spirit and lived in a body with a soul. Now Jesus is still a Man: Spirit, soul, and body. Except He now has a resurrected body since He rose from the dead.

Yes we are spirit, but God gave us a soul and body also. We are new creations in Christ (see 2 Cor. 5:17). Yes, we are spirit beings, but we are human beings too. All of our spirit, soul, and body need to come into alignment with the Kingdom of God—this only happens through the spirit first though. Paul wrote, *"Now may the God of peace Himself sanctify you entirely; and may your spirit and soul and body be preserved complete..."* (1 Thess. 5:23).

It is important that we as spirit, soul, and body blend as one so we can interact with the spiritual realm and the physical realm. Heaven was first a spiritual world. But then God created the earth and brought Heaven into it in the Garden of Eden. He brought Heaven into a physical dimension.

When you were born again, Christ came into your spirit, and in that seed is the fullness of the Godhead: Father, Son, and Holy Spirit. You are filled with eternity past, present, and future. *"But you have an anointing from the Holy One, and you know all things"* (1 John 2:20 NKJV).

Everything past, present, and future has already been written on the fabric of your spirit person. If you come into union with the Holy Spirit, you have access to know all things.

Many times while ministering, I will begin to see things through the impression of my mind in the spirit. I've learned that, when ministering in the Holy Spirit, I'm under the influence of the supernatural and that what's flowing into my mind is from Heaven. I've also learned that as I begin to speak in the natural about what I'm seeing in the spirit, it creates the framework for those things to be created in the natural.

Many years ago, Bob Jones was telling me about a time an angel woke him up and began to tell him about things he was to do. I stopped Bob and said, "Wait a minute Bob. What do you mean an angel came to you? Did you see him in the spirit or in the natural?"

I'll never forget what he told me. He leaned over in the chair and looked at me and said, "What's the difference?"

The reality of the spirit realm is all around us. Sometimes the Holy Spirit will just give you a hunch or a slight impression. But if you follow Him, you'll be surprised at what happens. Some of the most extraordinary miracles in your life will happen because you followed the tiniest nudge from the Holy Spirit.

Look to Heaven

When Abraham was an old man, God promised that his descendants would be like the stars. How was it possible for Abraham to become the father of two great nations? God told him to look into Heaven—to look at the stars. Abraham set his eyes to the heavens and looked. He imagined. He believed. This impossible situation became possible when he visualized it as a reality. As he looked at the stars, he saw his family.

God wants us to be active in our part of stepping into our destinies. God speaks the promise, but we fail to look up; we fail to visualize; we fail to see the impossible situation with eyes of faith. When we use our imaginations according to the promises of God, the impossible becomes possible.

In his book *Fourth Dimension,* Dr. Paul Yonggi Cho (David Cho) explains how the Holy Spirit incubated the earth when it was without form and substance as a physical planet. God also expects us to be active in the incubation of our faith by visualizing the final results of His promise. Dr. Cho says:

> My church has not grown to its present membership of 275,000 people because I am the most gifted pastor in the world. No. It has grown to its present size because I have followed Abraham's principle of visualization. In 1984, I see my church having half a million members. I can count them. I can see their faces in my heart.[2]

As of 2007, Dr. Cho's church has 830,000 members. I think he's on to something.[3]

God calls those things that are not as though they already exist. When the earth was formless and void, God already saw it with form and substance and simply called it forth. Our words must agree with our vision in order to bring them to pass. Paul said, "'...I believed, therefore I spoke,' we also believe, therefore we also speak" (2 Cor. 4:13).

If we see ourselves sick, broken down, and impoverished, that is exactly what will be birthed in our lives. If we begin to imagine ourselves as blessed of God and start calling those things that are not as though they are, they will manifest in our lives. Regardless of our race, gender, financial condition, or family situation we must believe and speak. Let's be like Abraham and look up at the stars.

Let It Be Done

> And when Jesus entered Capernaum, a centurion came to Him, imploring Him, and saying, "Lord, my servant is lying paralyzed at home, fearfully tormented." Jesus said to him, "I will come and heal him." But the centurion said, "Lord, I am not worthy for You to come under my roof, but just say the word, and my servant will be healed. For I also am a man under authority, with soldiers under me; and I say to this one, 'Go!' and he goes, and to another, 'Come!' and he comes, and to my slave, 'Do this!' and he does it." Now when Jesus heard this, He marveled and said to those who were following, "Truly I say to you, I have not found such **great faith** with anyone in Israel." ...And Jesus said to the centurion, "Go; **it shall be done for you as you have believed.**" And the servant was healed that very moment (Matthew 8:5-10,13).

From the above passage of Scripture, we can pull out several significant teachings on the topics of faith, believing, and healing, among many others. But the solitary lesson I want to draw from this passage is that of faith in relationship to our imagination. As we have talked about, I believe our imaginations are part of the creative nature of humanity.

Everything God spoke into existence already existed in His mind and in His heart. Everything that a person builds first lives within him—within the imagination.

We know that faith is not just a matter of the mind but of the heart. When God asks us to have faith in Him, He is asking us to trust Him. Trust is a matter of the heart. But true faith doesn't just stay in the heart; indeed, faith first springs from the heart, but it eventually floods the rest of the individual including the mind, imagination, and, in time, every action and word.

In the story of the faith of the centurion, we see Jesus saying that He will come to the centurion's servant to heal him. Jesus was perfectly fine with going the distance, but the centurion believed within himself that his servant would be healed if only Jesus spoke the word. The centurion's faith rested in the spoken word. Because he was a man of authority, a man of the spoken word, he had his mind made up and was firmly convinced in the authority of the spoken word. His faith was in the spoken word.

Look at Jesus' response in the New King James Version: *"Go your way; and as you have believed, so let it be done for you"* (Matt. 8:13 NKJV). It is in the way you believe, the way you imagine, and where your faith rests. For example, many people believe God is more likely to heal them of cancer in a Benny Hinn meeting than at a local church meeting. If that's where your faith rests, that's where you will be healed; by all means, get to that meeting. But if you are firmly convinced in your mind and heart that God can heal you through watching Benny Hinn on television, then you will be healed as you watch him in your living room. But if your faith rests in the healing Word of God, I'm sure you'll daily claim Isaiah 53:5 over yourself: *"By His stripes I am healed!"* Because imagination helps cultivate faith and belief, you could say, "As you imagine, it will be done unto you."

Another example of this in Scripture is the story of the woman with an issue of blood. This lady had a hemorrhage that was bleeding for 12 years, and after much medical help it only grew worse. This woman heard about Jesus, and when she finally saw Him, she knew that if she could touch the hem of his cloak she would be healed. Look at what she *thought*, or we could say *imagined: "After hearing about Jesus, she came up in the crowd behind Him and touched His cloak. For she **thought**, 'If I just touch His garments, I will get well'"* (Mark 5:27-28).

If anyone would have asked that woman what she wanted most in life, anytime during those 12 years, I bet she would have responded, "To be well." Everyday during those 12 years she *thought* about the day she would be better; she *imagined* being well again. Look at Jesus' response:

> *And a woman who had been suffering from a hemorrhage for twelve years, came up behind Him and touched the fringe of His cloak; for she was **saying to herself,** "If I only touch His garment, I will get well." But Jesus turning and seeing her said, "Daughter, take courage; **your faith has made you well"** (Matthew 9:20-22).*

Her faith made her well; her faith rested in touching the cloak of Jesus. She cultivated that faith by *imagining* and *saying* what she wanted.

I believe there is a special grace in this hour for us to engage the realm of Heaven. There has never been a better time to walk in the fullness of Christ. Paul says, *"...keep seeking the things above, where Christ is, seated at the right hand of God. Set you mind on the things above, not on the things that are on earth"* (Col. 3:1-2). As we fix our gaze on Jesus and keep seeking the things above with our minds and imaginations, we will get breakthrough—we will literally get to see the eternal realm. When we glimpse Jesus, everything will be changed. In this process, we must use our imaginations to reconstruct our entire thought lives. We must learn to take every thought captive to the obedience of Christ and set our affections on things above (see 2 Cor. 10:5). We will start to see ourselves and everyone around us through the eyes of Christ. We will start to *see* our destiny and our future Glory. Then, and only then, will we be able to pull it into today.

Language of Vision

*...that He may grant you a spirit of wisdom and revelation [of insight into mysteries and secrets] in the [deep and intimate] knowledge of Him. By having the eyes of your heart **flooded with light**, so that you can know and **understand** the hope to which He has called you, and how rich is His glorious inheritance in the saints (His set-apart ones)* (Ephesians 1:17-18 AMP).

The Greek word for "understanding" in the verse above is *dianoia* which properly means "to exercise your mind or imagination." Also, "flooded with light" in other Bible translations is "enlighten," which is the Greek word *photizo*, meaning "to brighten or illuminate," as in taking a picture; it's where we get our word photograph. The verse above is saying that the eyes of your understanding will be enlightened and illuminated as you exercise and engage your imagination.

Paul says, *"...for we walk by faith, not by sight"* (2 Cor. 5:7). True faith is seeing the unseen. Paul is saying that we walk, not by natural sight, but by seeing in the spirit. Jesus said, *"I tell [speak] the things which I have seen and learned at My Father's side..."* (John 8:38 AMP). Paul wrote,

*Since we consider and **look** not to the things that are seen but to the things that are **unseen;** for the things that are visible are temporal (brief and fleeting), but **the things that are invisible are deathless and everlasting** (2 Corinthians 4:18 AMP).*

We do this by looking with the eyes of our heart—with the eyes of our imagination. When we look with the eyes of understanding, we are gazing into the eternal realm—the real realm.

God can speak to us through the imagination, the devil can speak to us through the imagination, and we can use our own imagination. If we are imagining something from our own mind, it is coming from us. But imaginations that come from outside ourselves are coming from one of two sources: God or the devil. We can be imagining something from ourselves and then, all of a sudden, we receive something not from ourselves—something from God or the devil. "Where did that come from?" You might think, "I wasn't even thinking about that!" Because you were exercising your imagination, you were open to the spirit realm. The spirit realm loves to imprint pictures and thoughts into our imaginations because our imaginations are the gateway and the link that brings the spiritual into the natural.

If someone constantly receives ungodly images, they may just think it's their own imagination. In reality they actually have a demonic spirit lodged in their mind. That demonic spirit is the gatekeeper to the imagination; he guards what comes in and what goes out. Our spirit, as one with the Holy Spirit, should be the gatekeeper to our imaginations. This is why it's vital that our minds are washed with pure water so those strongholds in the mind and imagination can be broken and replaced (see Titus 3:5). When we find our mind wandering randomly and it leads us into perverseness, it's an indicator that there are strongholds in the mind and that we need deliverance. Deliverance is as simple as starving those strongholds and thoughts and having the powerful blood of Jesus Christ wash over us. We are the keepers of our minds; we must guard what comes into our eye-gates and ear-gates.

When daydreaming, either you started it or someone else did. The spirit world always wants to communicate with us. The vast majority of God's communication with people in the Scriptures came in visions and dreams. Napoleon believed that the imagination ruled the world; Einstein believed that the imagination was the world; the Bible tells us the imagination creates your world. Remember, as a person thinks in his heart, so he becomes (see Prov. 23:7).

Someone else has access to our minds other than us. Who is it? Learn to see for yourself. Accept the good and reject the evil. Train your mind and exercise your spiritual senses to discern the voice of God from among all the other voices (see Heb. 5:14). If you want to walk with God, you will have to learn to walk with Him in your imagination, having the eyes of your understanding enlightened that you may know the things of God.

The Key for Creativity

Webster's New World Dictionary defines the word *imagine* as "to make a mental image, to conceive in the mind, and to suppose and think." This is saying that we conceive and come up with ideas in the mind, which have no *tangible* or *touchable* foundation. It defines the word *imagination* as "the act or power of forming mental images of what is not present, and the act or power of creating new ideas." The imagination is our gift from God that should be used as a tool to create and manifest the unseen into the seen.

God has created us to be a thinking, imaginative, and visionary people who, with the sanctified imagination, like God, *"...calls into being that which does not exist"* (Rom. 4:17). God has given us the power to create, and not just through procreation or reproduction, but in many different ways including artistically and visually.

We are inventive and creative like our Father in Heaven. Every physical item that surrounds you right now, whether it's a clock, a picture frame, or a coffee cup, has a certain amount of imagination and creative design put into it. Every masterpiece ever created first existed in the imagination of the artist.

What's Your Vision?

Time and time again I hear pastors and leaders ask each other, "What's your vision for your church or ministry?" What they're saying is, "What do you envision? What do you imagine and see? What are you calling into existence and believing God to bring into present reality?"

It is important that we see ourselves the way God sees us. We are citizens of Heaven. We must be transformed from natural ways of thinking to heavenly ways. In Genesis 2:7, God breathed the breath of life into Adam and he became the first living *soul*. When God breathed the breath of life, He breathed all eternity into Adam—Adam's destiny, identity, citizenship, origin, imagination, and the Spirit of Wisdom and Understanding all came out of the eternity of eternities, directly out of God, and into Adam. Talk about an overdose.

> *For You formed my inward parts; You wove me in my mother's womb. I will give thanks to You, for I am fearfully and wonderfully made; wonderful are Your works, and my soul knows it very well. My frame was not hidden from You, when I was made in secret, and skillfully wrought in the depths of the earth; Your eyes have seen my unformed substance; and in Your book were all written the days that were ordained for me, when as yet there was not one of them. How precious also are Your thoughts to me, O God! How vast is the sum of them* (Psalm 139:13-17).

We are citizens of Heaven; our origin is not from here. We are the very offspring of God. Doesn't this tell us something of our ability to access the very home from which we came? We can use our imaginations to creatively bring into the natural that which exists in the spirit. We can release the will of God for our families, friends, ministries, businesses, cities, states, and the nations. So what's on your heart? What is your vision?

Sealed and Ordered

You have a blueprint and destiny from God within your spirit that's unchangeable. Most often the desires in our hearts are the very things God has *sealed* and *ordered* in us by the Holy Spirit. We are capable of bringing out and birthing our destinies. If we don't, we will agonize over it until it happens. Many of us wonder what the will of God is for our lives when it's already written all over us.

Visualizing

There are times when I'm alone with the Lord in the Spirit and I find myself visualizing and screaming out for the things I dream about: healing the masses in Africa, casting out demons with a word, God backing up my words with powerful signs and wonders. I imagine the Glory of God sweeping over a football field-sized amphitheater with Holy Spirit power and fire wiping out the whole place. I visualize the power of God covering a whole city, everybody getting saved, and miracles and healings being demonstrated in power by His radiant Glory! Then I listen to the people come into the great congregation of the Lord and testify of what great things God has done for them, person after person coming forward to testify.

These things will happen in my lifetime because I can see them! I've been to many of these events in the Spirit and they are wonderful. God has put it in me to call these things forth. They will happen, and I will be a part of facilitating these mighty acts of God. Proverbs says, *"Where there is no vision [no redemptive revelation of God], the people perish…"* (Proverbs 29:18 AMP). I'm going as far as to say that unless we visualize and give expression to these prophetic dreams and visions that come from the Holy One living inside us, we will begin to dry up on the vine and lose hope and courage. If that happens, eventually we might settle for far less than God's most perfect will for ourselves.

We've been told for too long that we can't use our imaginations to engage God. But I'm saying you can. You are free under the direction of the Holy Spirit to engage the third heavens and to uncover truths and mysteries in the Kingdom of God.

Engaging in Revelation

If we're hungry about moving in the same kinds of experiences Ezekiel or Isaiah had, we need to start meditating over their third Heaven experiences and start asking the Lord for our own. We need to take time to soak in the powerful presence of the Holy Spirit and use our imagination to engage Heaven based on what John saw in Revelation and what Daniel and Ezekiel and Isaiah saw. When we engage ourselves in this manner, it's only a matter of time before we are before the very throne of God ourselves. Remember, God is the Rewarder of those who diligently seek Him (see Heb. 11:6).

Unless we exercise our imaginations in a sanctified manner as God intended and take back the right to use our imaginations from the devil, we will be at a great disadvantage. God loves dreamers and visionaries who believe His Word. We need to get a hold of God and let Him get a hold of us. We need to shake Heaven until we see the full fruit of our heart's desires come to pass.

Endnotes

1.   Smith Wigglesworth, quoted in Stanley Howard Frodsham, *Smith Wigglesworth: Apostle of Faith* (Springfield, MO: Gospel Publishing House, 1948), www.smithwigglesworth.com/life/birth.htm (accessed March 24, 2009).

2.   David Yonggi Cho, *The Fourth Dimension, Volume Two* (Orlando, FL: Bridge-Logos, 1983), 60-61.

3.   "David Yonggi Cho," *Wikipedia,* www.en.wikipedia.org/wiki /David_Yonggi_Cho (accessed March 24, 2009).

CHAPTER 14

GLORY ATMOSPHERES

Have you ever been in a meeting where it seemed dry, like not much was going on, and then all of a sudden the atmosphere changed and was supercharged and ready to explode? More than likely it's because a heavenly portal opened up in the room. One of the glorious mysteries of the Kingdom is the existence of supernatural gates, windows, passageways, and heavenly doors. These are portals leading to and from the heavens where angels can come and go, moving up and down in the realm of Glory. When you're standing in a Glory portal, there is an open Heaven around you. A Glory portal is a "spherical opening of light" reaching between Heaven and earth, offering divine protection by which "angels and heavenly beings" can come and go without demonic interference.

I was doing a conference in Nashville several years ago with Bob Jones, and as Bob was prophesying over the people, a visible portal of light opened above. We even caught it on film. When these Glory portals open up, the angels are going up and down bringing supernatural flow for us.

James says, *"Every good gift and every perfect gift is from above, and comes down from the Father of lights"* (James 1:7 NKJV). Did you ever wonder what those "lights" are? I believe they are spiritual beings. They are Love; they are destiny; they are the "Great Cloud of Witnesses."

A few years ago, Jan and I were doing a conference in Parsons, Kansas, and during the ministry time lights began to streak across the sides of the building and across the top of the ceiling. These lights came all through the evening as the sun was setting. All the shades were shut with no light coming through. As we watched the lights they increased in activity until it looked like a laser light show. These angels came to do the works of the Lord.

Heavenly beings and the angels of God flow through spherical Glory portals as streams of love and light bringing revelation, power, strength, and healing virtue to the believer. These portals of Glory, or Glory dimensions, exist as supernatural pathways, doors, spheres, levels, or stages that unlock the process of revelation and its mysteries that are revealed and opened up to the believer by understanding. A Glory dimension is a higher world of thought. Glory dimensions are not far from us, but are right in front of us at all times. By understanding and decree, they open up as heavenly gates and establish Kingdom realities that manifest substance in our midst. Understanding alone won't open them up; we need to be speaking in faith what we see. Paul called them the heavenly realm.

> *May blessing (praise, laudation, and eulogy) be to the God and Father of our Lord Jesus Christ (the Messiah) Who has blessed us in Christ with every spiritual (given by the Holy Spirit) blessing in the **heavenly realm*** (Ephesians 1:3 AMP).

> *And He raised us up together with Him and made us sit down together [giving us joint seating with Him] in the*

*heavenly sphere [by virtue of our being] in Christ Jesus
(the Messiah, the Anointed One)* (Ephesians 2:6 AMP).

Heaven Around Us

Heaven is around us at all times, and when connected to like a radio frequency, it pulls that heavenly dimension into the natural and manifests it. The word spoken in faith brings a creative activation of substance in the realm of the spirit resulting in manifested miracles, healings, signs, and wonders.

Jesus told the disciples:

> *And as you go, preach, saying* [spoken word that brings Heaven], *"The Kingdom of Heaven is at hand!" Cure the sick, raise the dead, cleanse the lepers, drive out demons* (Matthew 10:7-8 AMP).

As they preached the spoken word pulled from the spirit world and manifested the Kingdom in the natural. My friend Tudor Bismark says, "God needs atmosphere to work with and it's crucial that we understand how to bring it. Praise changes the atmospheric conditions."[1]

> *But You are holy, O You Who dwell in [the holy place where] the praises of Israel [are offered]* (Psalm 22:3 AMP).

Jesus is *enthroned* upon the praises of His people. Jehoshaphat, King of Judah, led the people into battle against the Moabites and men of Ammon and Mount Seir that were without number. The singers and the priests were in front, leading the way into battle singing.

> *And when they began to sing and to praise, the Lord set ambushments against the men of Ammon, Moab, and Mount Seir who had come against Judah, and they were [self-] slaughtered* (2 Chronicles 20:22 AMP).

The atmosphere of praise and thanksgiving completely destroyed the works of the devil.

Establishing Atmosphere

Tudor also states:

> Atmosphere is created as the result of spiritual influence and pull whether good and bad. Once the spiritual influence is established that atmosphere when maintained over a prolonged period of time will create a spiritual climate.

God is calling us in this season to change the atmosphere into a spiritual climate.

> When climates are sustained and maintained whether good or bad over a prolonged period of time they create strongholds. Strongholds in turn bring about the belief systems that establish behavior in a society. [2]

It is these belief systems that create behavior. Satan is the master of atmosphere. He is the prince of the power of the air in Ephesians 2:2. We are all continually being influenced by atmosphere whether good or bad.

Adam walked with God and was always in Heaven because he was close to God. He exercised dominion over the earth and satan was under his feet. When we touch the *mind of Heaven,* we are in Heaven. Jesus said,

> ...the Kingdom of God is **within you** (Luke 17:21 AMP).

Heaven is closeness to God. As near as a thought. We change the atmosphere by speaking and releasing the prophetic decree into an atmosphere of Glory. Our words are powerful. When spoken in faith and full belief of the final outcome, our words contain the framework and creative power of Spirit and life to birth things in the physical. Jesus said the words He speaks are Spirit and Life (see John 6:63). God is bringing forth children that will move into the next level and fully manifest the Kingdom of power and Glory in the earth just as Jesus did, but we need to change the way we think. If a climate can be created and established that means it can be changed. If a climate can be created that means it can be sustained if conditions are maintained. Climates are prevalent at every level in society.

God created Adam and Eve and placed them in Eden as His family upon the earth. They walked with God every day, and He spoke with them as a father does with his children.

So when Adam and Eve sinned, there was a difference that was placed between them which caused separation with God. The climate in the garden was a powerful, creative environment where there was complete order with God, and whatever Adam needed he simply had to speak it into existence and he would have it. There was total harmony with the universe. It was one voice, one union, and one flow. When satan took authority he broke the harmony between God and humanity and then controlled the flow of power between them. He stepped between the Spirit and mind of God and the spirit and mind of humans and put distance between us.

God was as close as a whisper, but then an enormous gulf of separation was in the way. Rebellion entered the atmosphere and the climatic conditions were changed. Humans fell short of the Glory of God, which was the state of harmonious creative spiritual power in which they were created (see Rom. 3:23). No longer were they duel-dimensional individuals having access to the spirit world and the physical world at the same time. No longer did they have free access to Eden. No longer did they have unbroken fellowship with God. They were alienated from spirit power and forced to live the rest of their natural, physical lives in their mind, their five senses, and their own reasoning ability.

In a very short period of time, rebellion filled the earth and humanity was enslaved in the trenches of sin. The Bible says that God repented that He made humans (see Gen. 6:6). How did this happen? Satan changed the climatic conditions that prevailed in the earth.

Someone who listens to rebellious music irregardless of upbringing will eventually begin to take on the characteristics of what he's been listening to. Evil communications corrupt good behavior.

Proverbs says that what a person thinks in his mind or heart is what he becomes, both good and bad (see Prov. 23:7). Jesus said:

> ...*Be careful what you are hearing. The measure [of thought and study] you give [to the truth you hear] will be the measure [of virtue and knowledge] that comes back to you...* (Mark 4:24 AMP).

The Spoken Decree

We as believers have the ability to speak into the Glory and bring an atmosphere that changes the spiritual climate by the spirit of faith. The release of that spoken decree will open the spirit world and bring the Glory of God that will change the atmospheric condition. The Lord told Job:

> *You shall also decide and decree a thing, and it shall be established for you; and the light [of God's favor] shall shine upon your ways* (Job 22:28).

Glory comes when faith is released. It is then we can call things that are not as though they are by prophetic decree and they are created. Destinies are released, body parts are created and recreated, sickness is destroyed, finances are brought forth, ministries are birthed, and signs and wonders are performed that confirm the word. If the devil tells you that your body is riddled with sickness, don't agree with him. If he tells you that you are bankrupt, don't agree with him. Respond with the prophetic decree that by His stripes we are and were healed. We are the rich and not poor—the head and not the tail (see Deut. 28).

If we can agree with God touching any one thing on the earth, it can be birthed out of the realm of Glory. When we start creating with our words, the devil is in trouble. His world will crumble and cannot recover. We are then reclaiming and recreating the atmosphere and reclaiming what was lost in Eden.

Sustaining the Glory

Glory portals open up in the throne room, travel through the second heaven, and open up on the Earth. They open when drawn upon by faith. When faith pulls, then Heaven manifests at that place of our belief. Our job is to have faith and create spiritual hunger to establish an atmosphere for the Glory of God that will pull substance into the natural.

Getting the Glory to come is one thing, but creating an environment that will sustain the Glory is another. We can have powerful explosions of the Glory of God with miracles, but if we don't sustain that atmosphere of Glory in revival, we cannot change our churches, cities, states, regions, and nations. All authority has been given to Jesus in earth and Heaven (see Matt. 28:18). When we wake up and understand that we've been given all authority as the Body of Christ, we will then be able to take back control over the spiritual conditions of entire cities, regions, and nations. The world has been longing to see a people who not only claim to know God, but walk, talk, and act like Him.

> For God Who said, "Let light shine out of darkness," has shone in our hearts so as [to beam forth] the Light for the illumination of the knowledge of the majesty and glory of God [as it is manifest in the Person and is revealed] in the face of Jesus Christ (the Messiah) (2 Corinthians 4:6 AMP).

It is God's desire that the glorious Light and power of His presence would shine in and through a Glory generation of believers all across the globe. But in order for us to bring Heaven to earth, we must first bring earth to Heaven. The word of the Lord to the Church now is *"Come up to the mountain and I will show you My ways and teach you My paths"* (see Ex. 20:12; Ps. 25:4) But that's another chapter. Throughout Scripture, we see the existence of doorways or Glory portals:

> *Lift up your heads, O you gates! And be lifted up, you everlasting doors! And the King of glory shall come in* (Psalm 24:7 NKJV).

> *He had commanded the clouds above, and opened the doors of Heaven* (Psalm 78:23 NKJV).

> *Blessed is the man who listens to me, watching daily at my gates, waiting at the posts of my doors* (Proverbs 8:34 NKJV).

> *…Most assuredly, I say to you, hereafter you shall see Heaven open, and the angels of God ascending and descending upon the Son of Man* (John 1:51 NKJV).

> *After these things I looked, and behold, a door standing open in Heaven. And the first voice which I heard was like a trumpet speaking with me, saying "Come up here, and I will show you things which must take place after this." Immediately I was in the spirit…* (Revelation 4:1-2 NKJV).

The "door" in Revelation suggests God's invitation for us to come up to His heavenly realm. As His friends, the Lord wants to open the portals of Heaven and release an unparalleled visitation of heavenly hosts. It is not just Heaven coming down, but us going up.

Jacob Finds a Door

Jacob spent the night in a place where his forefather Abraham had called upon the name of the Lord (see Gen. 28:16-17). As he rested his head upon a covenant stone, a portal or a heavenly door opened. Jacob saw a vision of a ladder with angels ascending and descending on it. When he awoke from sleep, he said:

> ...*Surely the Lord is in this place, and I did not know it....How awesome is this place! This is none other than the house of God, and this is the gate of Heaven* (Genesis 28:16-17 NKJV).

Jacob marked the stairway to Heaven and named the place "Bethel," or "dwelling place of God." Several times after this, the Lord told Jacob to return to Bethel where He would speak to him further. Have you ever wondered why the Lord, who could speak to a person anywhere, would instruct Jacob to go back to Bethel so He could speak with him further? Bethel was a literal portal. This is the same place the Lord led Abraham to sacrifice Isaac. It is a designated place by God for communication between Heaven and earth. God told Elijah to eat angel cake that would give him strength to get him to the portal of Mount Horeb. While God was talking to Elijah, He instructed the prophet to go to Mount Horeb, also known as Mount Sinai, where the Lord would talk to him further:

> As he [Elijah] *lay asleep under the broom or juniper tree, behold, an angel touched him and said to him, "Arise and eat." He looked, and behold, there was a cake baked on the coals, and a bottle of water at his*

head. And he ate and drank and lay down again. The angel of the Lord came the second time and touched him and said, "Arise and eat, for the journey is too great for you." So he arose and ate and drank, and went in the strength of that food forty days and nights to Horeb, the mount of God (1 Kings 19:5-8 AMP).

Divine portals into the heavenly realm exist around the earth today. The city of Jerusalem is a portal. In fact, it is the major portal on the face of the earth. That's why both David and Isaiah said that Jerusalem is the center of the earth. The occult and the kingdom of darkness understand the reality of dark portals in the spirit as well and guard them with great fervor. I've been told of great battles that church leaders in the United States, who actually purchased property to build their churches on, have gone through. Many of them had to fight for existence as it seemed all hell had come against them.

One pastor told me he actually had a member from the church of satan come to him in California and say, "You know we mean to kill you. You planted your church on our lay line." A lay line is a demonic portal dedicated to satan as territory for him. Demonic portals open up much the same way as heavenly portals do, where demons can come and go from the spirit realm to the natural. With great faith this church prevailed and overcame the situation.

God is calling His people to take back these high places so that His angels can come and go without hindrance. Begin to take authority and establish the atmosphere of Heaven everywhere your feet tread. You have power to dictate and decree a thing so it will be established—start decreeing daily to create Glory atmospheres everywhere you go.

Endnotes

1. Tudor Bismark, *Dimensions, Atmospheres and Climates,* audio teaching (www.jabula.org).

2. Ibid.

CHAPTER 15

REDISCOVERING THE ANCIENT PATHWAYS

*This is what the Lord says: "Stand at the crossroads and look; ask for the **ancient paths,** ask where the good way is, and walk in it, and you will find rest for your souls* (Jeremiah 6:16 NIV).

*But My people are not so reliable, for they have deserted Me; they burn incense to worthless idols. They have stumbled off the **ancient highways** and walk in muddy paths* (Jeremiah 18:15 NLT).

*Thus says the Lord God: "Because the enemy has said over you, 'Aha!' and, 'The **ancient heights** have become our possession'"* (Ezekiel 36:2 AMP).

*Whom Heaven must receive [and retain] until the time for the complete restoration of all that God spoke by the mouth of all His holy prophets for ages past [from the most **ancient time** in the memory of man]* (Acts 3:21 AMP).

Jesus Walked the Ancient Pathways

Jesus walked the Ancient Pathways with God and chose to follow them even unto death, opening up for us a new and living way that leads us back home to the Father. Jesus opened up the "Way" through the veil of His flesh. He offered Himself willingly to bring us back to God. He told Mary in the garden after the resurrection, *"...I am ascending to My Father and your Father, and to My God and your God"* (John 20:17 AMP). In order to get back to Eden we need to walk the way Jesus walked. His was a life of contemplation, prayer, devotion, and communion with the Father. Thomas said, "Lord, we do not know where You are going, so how can we know the way?" Jesus said, *"I am the Way and the Truth and the Life; no one comes to the Father except by (through) Me"* (see John 14:5-6).

After Adam fell from the Glory of God, the Lord God placed a cherubim with a flaming sword to keep and guard "the way" to the tree of life:

> *And the Lord God said, "Behold, the man has become like one of Us [the Father, Son, and Holy Spirit], to know [how to distinguish between] good and evil and blessing and calamity; and now, lest he put forth his hand and take also from the tree of life and eat, and live forever—" Therefore the Lord God sent him forth from the Garden of Eden to till the ground from which he was taken. So [God] drove out the man; and He placed at the east of the Garden of Eden the cherubim and a flaming sword which turned every way, to keep and guard the way to the tree of life* (Genesis 3:22-24 AMP).

Jesus opened the ancient pathway by offering Himself as a living sacrifice to God. He Himself said, *"I am the way"* (see John 14:6). The way back to what? The way back to Eden. For through a man, death came to all of humankind. So by one Man all are made alive:

> *For since [it was] through a man that death [came into the world, it is] also through a Man that the resurrection of the dead [has come]. For just as [because of their union of nature] in Adam all people die, so also [by virtue of their union of nature] shall all in Christ be made alive* (1 Corinthians 15:21-22 AMP).

Adam had borne the image of God and was created from the dust of the earth. He enjoyed blissful friendship with the Lord, walking and talking daily with Him as a father would enjoy his son. Our relationship to God was cut off, but Jesus, the "Heavenly Man," opened up the ancient roads once again as One who bears the image of a heavenly Man. Jesus became a "Life-Giving Spirit" and restored humankind back to the place from which we fell.

> *Thus it is written, "The first man Adam became a living being (an individual personality)"; the last Adam (Christ) became a life-giving Spirit [restoring the dead to life]. But it is not the spiritual life which came first, but the physical and then the spiritual. The first man [was] from out of earth, made of dust (earthly-minded); the second Man [is] the Lord from out of Heaven. Now those who are made of the dust are like him who was first made of the dust (earthly-minded); and as is [the Man] from Heaven, so also [are those] who are of Heaven (heavenly-minded). And just as we have borne the image [of the man] of dust, so shall we and so let us also bear the image [of the Man] of Heaven* (1 Corinthians 15:45-49 AMP).

Enoch Walked the Ancient Pathways

Enoch walked with God on the ancient pathways and was no more, for God took him (see Gen. 5:22-24). Enoch spent so much time on these supernatural highways that God finally kept him. Enoch walked in the heavenlies with the Lord and knew the vast resources of that place with all its limitless dimensions in the spirit realm. He was even asked to make amends between the fallen angels and the Creator.[1] As a forerunner, Enoch was granted permission to see things few had seen. Obviously, Adam was still alive during Enoch's time on earth, and I'm certain Enoch spent much of his time speaking with him about what it was like before the Fall. I can imagine Adam sharing with Enoch how he walked with the Lord in the Garden, moving with effortless authority. Having this knowledge to draw from, Enoch had an anchor to approach God with.

With the help of the angels, God granted Enoch access into His presence. He moved on the ancient pathways originally designed for humankind. His relentless quest to know God opened the heavens that were shut off to most. God is a Rewarder to those who hotly pursue Him. He wrote down many of his revelations and encounters in the heavenly realms. They are recorded in the "Book of Enoch." It was quite clear that the early church had and quoted the book of Enoch and highly valued it. Jesus, Peter, and Jude all cited passages from it. Even though it is not considered Canon, it is like other documented chronicles detailing Enoch's travels to Heaven and his communications with the Lord.

The Heart of God

From the beginning of time, God has always longed for a people that would be completely His—a family in the earth that He could share His heart and the secrets of the universe with. Knowing the beginning from the end it was an act worthy of pursuit, knowing there would one day be a people that would not turn their back on Him or push Him away. After being delivered from Egypt through incredible signs and wonders, the children of Israel had been offered an invitation as a nation to come up on the mountain and see the Glory of God as Moses did. God was wanting all of His children to know Him and shine with His Glory as Moses did, but instead, after being prepared three days, they turned the invitation of the Lord down because they were afraid of His presence.

In the third month after the Israelites left the land of Egypt, the same day, they came into the Wilderness of Sinai....And Moses went up to God, and the Lord called to him out of the mountain, "Say this to the house of Jacob and tell the Israelites: 'You have seen what I did to the Egyptians, and how I bore you on eagles' wings and brought you to Myself. Now therefore, if you will obey My voice in truth and keep My covenant, then you shall be My own peculiar possession and treasure from among and above all peoples; for all the earth is Mine. And you shall be to Me a kingdom of priests, a holy nation [consecrated, set apart to the worship of God].'"...And the Lord said to Moses, "Go and sanctify the people [set them apart for God] today and tomorrow, and let them wash their clothes and be ready by the third day, for the third day the Lord will come down upon Mount Sinai [in the cloud] in the sight of all the people....No hand shall touch it [or the offender], but he shall surely be stoned or shot (with arrows); whether beast or man, he shall not live. When the trumpet sounds a long blast, they shall come up to the mountain....The third morning there were thunders and lightnings, and a thick cloud upon the mountain, and a very loud trumpet blast, so that all the people in the camp trembled. Then Moses brought the people from the camp to meet God, and they stood at the foot of the mountain. Mount Sinai was wrapped in smoke, for the Lord descended upon it in fire; its smoke ascended like that of a furnace, and the whole mountain quaked greatly. As the trumpet blast grew louder and louder, Moses spoke and God answered him with a voice. The Lord came down upon Mount Sinai to the top of the mountain, and the Lord called Moses to the top of the mountain, and Moses went up (Exodus 19:1-20 AMP).

The invitation was for all of Israel to come on the mountain into the Glory of God, seeing His Glory and being transformed in His presence. But fear caused them to shy away. They refused God for fear of dying on the mountain:

Now all the people perceived the thunderings and the lightnings and the noise of the trumpet and the smoking mountain, and as [they] looked they trembled with fear and fell back and stood afar off. And they said to Moses, "You speak to us and we will listen, but let not God speak to us, lest we die." And Moses said to the people, "Fear not; for God has come to prove you, so that the [reverential] fear of Him may be before you, that you may not sin." And the people stood afar off, but Moses drew near to the thick darkness where God was (Exodus 20:18-21 AMP).

The Lord wanted all of His people to shine with His Glory like Moses. They had seen the power of His signs and wonders and how God had crushed the strongest nation on the planet, delivering them from bondage with raw supernatural authority never witnessed before. Seeing all these things, they still refused His invitation to come up into the mountain of His presence. They were just too afraid of the power of His majesty.

Not too much further down the road, Moses had sent out ten spies to search out the land God had sworn to give the Israelites as an inheritance for them. The spies were gone forty days scouting the land. When they returned they brought fruit from the Promised Land. One cluster alone from the valley of Eshcol was so large it had to be carried by two men on a pole due of the enormity of its size. Joshua and Caleb immediately reported to Moses and the people,

> *Caleb quieted the people before Moses, and said, "Let us go up at once and possess it [the land]; we are well able to conquer it." But his fellow scouts said, "We are not able to go up against the people [of Canaan], for they are stronger than we are." So they brought the Israelites an evil report of the land which they had scouted out, saying, "The land through which we went to spy it out is a land that devours its inhabitants. And all the people that we saw in it are men of great stature. There we saw the Nephilim [or giants], the sons of Anak, who come from the giants; and we were in our own sight as grasshoppers, and so we were in their sight* (Numbers 13:30-33 AMP).

So the people were afraid to enter the land for fear of the giants. They talked about choosing for themselves a new captain and returning to the land of Egypt. But Moses and Aaron fell on their faces before all the assembly of the Israelites. Joshua and Caleb tried to quiet the people and talk sense to them, saying:

> *If the Lord delights in us, then He will bring us into this land and give it to us, a land flowing with milk and honey. Only do not rebel against the Lord, neither fear the people of the land, for they are bread for us* (Numbers 14:8-9).

The congregation wouldn't hear what Joshua and Caleb had to say. They had made up their minds. They were going to stone Joshua and Caleb with stones and make a plan to return to the land of Egypt.

But right in the middle of their meeting God showed up at the Tent of Meeting.

> But all the congregation said to stone [Joshua and Caleb] with stones. But the glory of the Lord appeared at the Tent of Meeting before all the Israelites. And the Lord said to Moses, "How long will this people provoke (spurn, despise) Me? And how long will it be before they believe Me [trusting in, relying on, clinging to Me], for all the signs which I have performed among them? I will smite them with the pestilence and disinherit them, and will make of you [Moses] a nation greater and mightier than they." But Moses said to the Lord, "Then the Egyptians will hear of it, for You brought up this people in Your might from among them. And they will tell it to the inhabitants of this land. They have heard that You, Lord, are in the midst of this people [of Israel], that You, Lord, are seen face to face, and that Your cloud stands over them, and that You go before them in a pillar of cloud by day and in a pillar of fire by night. Now if You kill all this people as one man, then the nations that have heard Your fame will say, 'Because the Lord was not able to bring this people into the land which He swore to give to them, therefore He has slain them in the wilderness.' And now, I pray You, let the power of my Lord be great, as You have promised, saying, 'The Lord is long-suffering and slow to anger, and abundant in mercy and loving-kindness, forgiving iniquity and transgression; but He will by no means clear the guilty, visiting the iniquity of the fathers upon the children, upon the third and fourth generation.' Pardon, I pray You, the iniquity of this people according to the greatness of Your mercy and loving-kindness, just as You

have forgiven [them] from Egypt until now (Numbers 14:10-19 AMP).

The Earth Shall Be Filled

The Lord was so upset with the children of Israel that He told Moses He was going to destroy them all with pestilence and disinherit them and make from Moses a nation greater and mightier than they. But Moses pleaded Israel's case to God, and God listened to Moses. But hear the thing God said:

And the Lord said, "I have pardoned according to your word. But truly as I live and as all the earth shall be filled with the glory of the Lord" (Numbers 14:20-21 AMP).

The Lord had had enough of these people. They had seen His Glory; they had witnessed His might, power, and strength. There had never been another nation that God had claimed for His own and had fought for. These people were eyewitnesses to His majesty, and though they literally walked through the Red Sea on dry ground, being led by the supernatural cloud by day and the pillar of fire by night, they still refused to believe that God was able to drive out the giants in the land and give them rest. The Lord told Moses these people are "stiff-necked." They refused to believe. God was so angry He would have killed them all as one man if it weren't for Moses. The Lord told Moses, "I have pardoned their sin according to your word, but truly *as I live and as all the earth shall be filled with the glory of the Lord!*"

God swore by His own Name that the earth would be filled with His Glory. He would have a people that would not refuse Him, a family in the earth, that know His ways and His paths—a supernatural people that know His Glory. This was the reason the Lord was angry with Israel. He revealed Himself over and over again to a stiff-necked people that chose not to believe in Him.

In the history of humankind, there has never been a generation of people to be filled with the Glory of the Lord, and I believe we are this generation. We are the Glory generation! I believe we are the people God was looking for, who will reveal the knowledge of the Glory of the Lord in the earth.

> *But [the time is coming when] the earth shall be filled with the knowledge of the glory of the Lord as the waters cover the sea* (Habakkuk 2:14 AMP).

There is a rising Glory generation already shining with the radiance and splendor of His light. This body will not just have faith in God but will have the faith *of* God. They will look and act like God in the earth. They will understand that they too are filled with the fullness of the Godhead—Father, Son, and Holy Spirit—and the Spirit of Holiness and resurrection power lives in them. They will become the gateway of God in the earth allowing Heaven to open up on them as Kingdom representatives. With this authority, they are able to act on God's behalf, destroying the works of the devil and establishing the will of Jesus everywhere they go. They will be filled with revelation knowledge, knowing how to implement righteousness and justice on the earth as God's magistrates and judiciaries. This is the rising Glory generation God was looking for. This is His Body on the earth.

Yes, it's true—Jesus Christ is coming back in the clouds one day, at the last day trump, but before that day He is coming back in and through a corporate Body of Christ in the earth. Jesus paid the ultimate price to restore us to right relationship with Himself, and now He is reaping the fruit of tears sown in the Garden of Gethsemane. For they who sow in tears will doubtless come again rejoicing, bringing in the sheaves. Jesus Christ paid a high price in blood to restore us to this place. The fruit is ripe in the ear and ready for harvest. Now is the time. Jesus has opened up the way back to Eden; He is the Tree of Life.

Endnote

1. Translated by R.H. Charles, *The Book of Enoch, Book 1: The Watchers,* http://www.ancienttexts.org/library/ethiopian/enoch/index .html (accessed March 26, 2009), Chapters 13-15.

SOAKING VIDEO (SV) SERIES

Acceleration into the Glory of God

More titles available through:

GLOBAL FIRE MINISTRIES
PMB 11
425 North Thompson Lane
Murfreesboro, TN 37129

E-mail: info@globalfireministries.com
Website: www.globalfireministries.com
Phone Number: 1 (615) 867-1124